THE CAUSES OF INSTABILITY IN NIGERIA AND IMPLICATIONS FOR THE UNITED STATES

Nigeria represents the best and worst of what African states offer the world. It is a mosaic of over 250 different ethnic groups and languages enriched as a crossroads between various forms of Christianity, Islam, and indigenous beliefs, and Western, Arab, and native influences. Its large area holds productive agricultural land and immense deposits of oil and natural gas rated at 10th and 8th largest, respectively, in world reserves.[1] Nigeria possesses international political clout through its strong military forces and active role in peace operations, as well as its recognized diplomatic leadership in international organizations like: the Organization of the Islamic Conference (OIC); Organization of Petroleum Exporting Countries (OPEC); as a founding member in the African Union (AU); and, the Economic Community of West African States (ECWAS).[2] Its population of 174 million also makes it by far the largest state in Africa and the 7th most populous in the world.[3] Nigeria is a land blessed.

Nigeria also demonstrates many of the problems that plague much of Africa's stability and progress. Nigerians have routinely endured strife along their many internal differences, from the bloody 1967-70 civil war to the one million Nigerians displaced by internal turmoil between 1999 and 2004.[4] Its larder of natural resources brings in much needed foreign revenue, but is a vast source of corruption, internecine conflict, and degradation to the environment and agricultural livelihoods. Its history since independence in 1960 has been tossed by political tumult with numerous military coups and autocratic governments, four

1

different republics, and a poor human rights record. Such problems have hobbled economic, social, and human development in Nigeria, which suffers a low gross domestic product (GDP) per capita (purchasing power parity) of $2,500 (175th in the world), literacy rate of only 61 percent, life expectancy of 47.6 years (220th in the world), and poverty rate at 70 percent, all making Nigeria one of the 20 poorest countries per capita in the world.[5] The country is noted as a hub for cyber crimes, drug and human trafficking, piracy, and nascent native extremism, as well as disease and general human suffering.[6] Nigeria is a troubled land.

This paradox of a nation offers much to its citizens and the world, but Nigeria has been unable to deliver on its potential or realize its aspirations.[7] Although currently in a positive trend of strong economic growth and improving democratic resiliency, the fundamental problems that have challenged Nigerian progress throughout its history remain simmering. These problems have been ascribed to many complex causes, including its colonial legacy, international intrigue, poverty, and cultural and religious conflicts, that leave Nigeria sometimes tottering at the edge of instability and liable to fracturing. However, the root cause for these and other problems may be the result of the political economy of Nigeria and the resulting centrifugal and centripetal forces that hold Nigeria as a unified state in the balance. To test this assertion, this monograph will first explain the definition of political economy employed here; why Nigeria wavers sometimes on the edge of failing as a state through the negative interaction of competing economics, politics, and societies; and the resulting rampant corruption and ossified fault lines that could splinter the state. It then makes modest recommendations for the

U.S. Government, and the U.S. military in particular, to assist Nigerians in attaining the stability needed to remain a functioning, integrated state. With its large population, ethnic tapestry, rich economic potential, diplomatic clout, and military strength, Nigeria remains an important regional power in Africa with increasing influence in international affairs. According to both the Departments of Defense (DoD) and State (DoS) in their 2010 engagement activities report to Congress:

> U.S. engagement with Nigeria on political, economic, and security issues is vital to the stability and prosperity of West Africa and the entire continent.[8]

Nigeria is thus worthy of serious U.S. efforts at understanding and assistance.

THE POLITICAL ECONOMY OF A STATE IN TURMOIL

In the daily routines of citizens and states alike, politics, economics, and culture are strong interrelated influencers. These are each encompassed in the useful term "political economy," which is concerned with the "interconnection of economic and political structures in social formation."[9] The central use of political economy in this study considers the mutual influence of economic activities and policies on politics and its ideologies, cultural and historic factors, and the self-interests of affected groups.[10] These broad interlocking concepts include several elements of the political economy that support this analysis, including formation of self-interested group action, redistribution of public economic gain, effects of cultural background,

3

and reform and development in the political, economic, and social aspects of Nigeria. The economy in terms of its benefits and rewards, as they are influenced by political and social activities and organizations, is the focus of this monograph.

Despite its daunting intricacies, the political economy is a rather self-evident concept. By our nature, human beings want to influence those things of most significance to us. Economic well-being ranks high in importance in meeting human needs, so it is not surprising that political and cultural associations would be formed to influence economic outcomes to benefit an individual or group. Indeed, classic economists like Adam Smith and David Ricardo primarily addressed political economy issues in their works. It was not until the 1880s that politics and economics were divorced in the continuing effort to quantify economics free of the taint of outside influences to create "an independent sphere of economics where politics didn't intrude and that mathematics allowed markets to be predictable. . . ."[11] The linkage of these forces in human endeavors is undeniable, however, which explains why a serious examination of turmoil afflicting a state like Nigeria must rely on this inexact but encompassing concept. Therefore, political and social involvement in economic affairs should be expected, and economic results will in turn affect them.[12] The political economy may be the most important, although certainly not the only, factor in explaining a state's current and future prosperity and stability.[13]

Because they are so fundamental to the well-being of humans, the distribution of power and economic gains may be the most volatile of intrastate problems. Under conditions of robust equitable per capita eco-

4

nomic growth, intrastate political and social rivalries are rare or can be ignored so as to not upset the shared benefits of growth. This situation occurred during the boom days of Yugoslavia, when one of Europe's fastest growing economies in the 1950s and 1960s overshadowed the interethnic and political turmoil that killed 750,000 Yugoslavs (through internecine fighting alone) during World War II. When relative standards of living decline or are inequitable, however, conditions often deteriorate, and problems manifest themselves as political or cultural cleavages in zero-sum pursuit of diminishing economic gains. Such was the case of the Yugoslav economic decline of the 1980s following international oil shocks and poor government policies that ultimately led to the political, cultural, and regional clashes that fractured Yugoslavia during the 1990s.[14] The examples of Yugoslavia and states like Sudan are instructive to the situation in Nigeria today.

Through most of its history, Nigeria's economy has woefully underperformed, with the resulting expected competition along a variety of traditional and modern self-interest groups. From independence in 1960 to 2000, Nigeria's income per capita stagnated in terms of purchasing power parity (PPP) despite the income per capita from petroleum, Nigeria's dominating source of income, increasing tenfold.[15] The country's per capita GDP (at the official exchange rate)[16] dropped from a high of $1,500 during the 1970s to a low of $300 in 1998, doubling the poverty rate to 70 percent.[17] By 2010, the GDP nearly recovered to $1,470, but poverty still remained at 70 percent, signaling serious inequity problems.[18] Analysis of 2010 communal clashes by a Nigerian professor in the chronically violence-prone central city of Jos noted a combination of political economic factors, including social apathy, economic

5

deprivation, and political frustration: "[I]t's simply an exhibition of the failure of governance in Nigeria; it's an exhibition of a very serious economic problem that Nigerians find themselves in." He goes on to observe that "too often in the midst of serious economic crisis, people often lose sight of the real problem to exploit the most visible difference between groups, in the case of Jos, the religious difference."[19] As this one example and the rest of this monograph will show, Nigeria's frequent and bloody turmoil throughout its history is often a result of manipulated groups clashing for a bigger share of an inadequately sized pie.

This poor record of economic development in Nigeria, despite its potential, is in large part due to two political economic causes which help to explain why economic policies have not fared better. The first is the inability of its leaders to meld a unified nation out of the "fragmented geographic and ethnic components" in Nigeria. The second is the unstable government structure from colonial to alternating elected and authoritarian regimes, with numerous military coups and different forms of governments.[20] Nigerians did not possess a strong sense of unity before or during the colonial period, which discouraged a sense of nationhood; indeed, British authorities may have actively pursued playing groups against each other.[21] Economic development was also not seriously stressed in colonial times beyond infrastructure development needed to exploit native resources and markets for imperial interests.[22] Since independence, demagogic politicians have sought to gain regional, ethnic, and confessional group support for their own interests and have severely divided Nigeria's society and polity. Self-determination, a method used by minorities to mobilize against central authority and leverage their position for concessions, is a common tactic in Nigerian politics and was taken to its limit in the unsuccessful secession of Biafra during the 1967-70 civil war.[23] Nigeria's wealth continues to be seen as a source of exploitation by its elite, often pitting groups against each other in pursuit of controlling national wealth.[24] In these ways, historic and modern economic, political, and social forces have influenced each other, resulting in a chronically weakened state.

The Political Economy in a Nigerian Rentier State.

Many of Nigeria's problems can be traced to its political economy because it represents the bread-and-butter issues that may sow internal disharmony. The country's policies have unbalanced the economy into one that depends highly upon exporting energy resources, which become the lucrative target of political economic infighting. The effects of a single product economy have encouraged self-serving actions by Nigerian citizens and organizations; fostered dependence on easy economic gains; and made the government overly centralized, unresponsive to its citizens, and corrupt. This section addresses Nigeria's economy and explains how it has become the foundation for so many other problems and a chronic distraction in U.S.-Nigerian relations.[25]

Nigeria's huge population, many resources, and favorable location produced a large economy that has integrated into the greater global economy through the centuries. Nigeria ranked 31st in the world in national GDP PPP, with $419 billion in 2011, and a healthy growth rate averaging above 7 percent since 2003.[26] The high price of petroleum over that period accounts for much of the wealth, since oil produces

25 percent of Nigeria's GDP and 80 percent of its government budget revenues.[27] Petroleum has taken over modern Nigeria's economy, rocketing from just 1 percent of GDP in 1960 to 26 percent in 1970. By 1976, oil dominated Nigeria's exports at 94 percent, remaining at 95 percent of foreign exchange earnings in 2011.[28] By comparison, Nigeria's economic output during the 1960s was 61 percent agricultural and was the cultural base of many ethnic groups.[29] The manufacturing sector, employing traditional skills and native products, was growing to a high of 11 percent of GDP in the 1970s before falling to just half that amount in 2000 and continuing to decline since.[30] In 2011, the agricultural sector employed 70 percent of Nigeria's labor force and was 35 percent of its GDP, but it accounted for only 4 percent of exports, while manufacturing accounted for only 1 percent of its GDP.[31] Foreign enclave energy production has entirely changed the basis of Nigeria's economy and collection of government revenues, and it has "undemocratized" its economy and tax base in the process.

The consequences of the oil boom in Nigeria and subsequent economic fallout is a classic example of "Dutch disease," in which an economic boon, often coming from a natural resource, has the unwanted effect of expanding a country's prices and thereby depressing local production and nonresource exports through indirectly subsidizing cheaper imports—all of which hampers growth.[32] Although a country as large and diverse as Nigeria has considerable influence over its economy through government policies,[33] Nigeria has consistently mismanaged its bonanza. A common consequence of Dutch disease makes the economy depend more upon a single commodity or sector and thus is prone to buffeting by international markets during unpredictable boom and bust cycles. In Nigeria, this is exacerbated by implementing expedient short-term solutions over long-term development.[34] Also, high economic growth spurred by oil production has been unable to pace Nigeria's staggering population growth, which nearly quadrupled from 46 million in 1960 to 174 million in 2013, with an average of 5.4 children born to each woman of child-bearing age today.[35] Nigeria's chronic case of Dutch disease was contracted through a combination of misguided and self-centered actions by the government, individuals, and mutually suspicious interest groups that have been unable to overcome partisanship.

Nigeria's cycle of disruptive and violent intergroup competition was paved in part with good intentions and unintended consequences. Starting in the late-1960s, the Nigerian government curtailed the amount of impartial technical advice it received by disbanding its core of international economic advisers.[36] One outcome of this action was that it tried "to do too much too soon, leaving the government administratively overextended."[37] Parts of the massive Nigerian government borrowing that followed went to finance "lavish, often superfluous" factory construction and poorly conceived prestige projects of dubious need that suffocated private enterprise.[38] Nigerian producers were also undermined by a currency inflated with oil earnings, which greatly increased the importing of consumables at the expense of locally produced goods.[39] Natural resource extraction absorbed nearly all foreign, private, and public investment, creating chronic rural underinvestment in the agricultural sector and its related infrastructure.[40] Another unexpected effect was that energy production jobs diverted skilled and unskilled labor from manufacturing and agricultural pursuits.[41] These negative effects of mis-allocating resources are classic symptoms of Dutch disease. Another secondary consequence was the serious environmental damage from extractive industries (including coal and tin) that directly damaged agricultural and aquatic pursuits and the livelihoods of Nigeria's poorest people, creating the unwanted effect of inciting crime and insurgency among the disaffected.[42]

Beyond the misallocation of funds, other government policies inadvertently hurt Nigeria's economic development.[43] During the boom years, Nigerian officials allowed the official currency exchange rate to appreciate and then kept it artificially overvalued when oil prices fell.[44] The dire results of this monetary policy were to depress native production of goods, fuel inflation, and encourage black market activities.[45] This policy crowded out other economic activities like agriculture and manufacturing, which could not play a sufficient role to counterbalance the effect of cyclical declines in oil revenue on the world economy. To smooth the troughs of international oil price fluctuations and to leverage export income during good times, Nigeria borrowed heavily from foreign sources, causing deep indebtedness and increased exposure to the dictates of crediting countries and organizations when those debts could not be paid.[46] The large expansion of government employment also diverted talent from other economic endeavors and increased wage rates added to inflationary pressure.[47] Through lack of vision or corrupt intent, Nigeria's leaders have failed to diversify its economy or maintain its infrastructure, to the serious detriment of the economy.[48] Despite the disbanding of the international advisors group, Nigerian officials may have understood the nature of these criticized economic policies. However, they were constrained by political pressure from their highly fractured constituents, who were maximizing their share in an underperforming economy.[49] For many reasons, the economic sectors in which the large majority of Nigerians work receive much less support from public investment and policy than that given to the highly concentrated extractive sector; yet proceeds from these natural resource based industries do not increase the general welfare of the population nor compensate them for their losses.[50] In Nigeria, these represent political decisions with far ranging economic and social consequences.

In addition to poor decisions and constrained options, other, baser, reasons also explain Nigeria's underperforming economy. Since the rents from the resource sector usually go to the government, Thomas Friedman's "curse of oil" posits how Nigerian autocrats misuse the state's wealth because they hold control over its rich natural resources — freeing them from accountability to their citizens; this was probably an underlying motive of the civil war.[51] The quality of a state's institutions, whether prone to being "grabber-friendly or producer-friendly . . . is the key to understanding the resource curse: when institutions are bad, resource abundance is a curse. . . ."[52] Throughout history, Nigerian administrations and their regional, cultural, religious, political, and economic associations consistently have been grabber-friendly. Dutch disease also increases the occurrence of corruption.[53] In one example, the regime of General Yakubu Gowan, which presided over the oil boom of the 1960s and 1970s, saw the oil windfall as a source of patronage through economic policies like import-substitution that could reward political allies "through gross misuse of the oil. . . ."[54] From 1988 to

1993, an official government report found $13 billion, or 20 percent of total revenues, were "sidetracked to off-budget accounts" that were entirely unmonitored and undermined economic growth. Within 2 years of that 1994 report, the regime of General Sani Abacha diverted 17 percent of Nigeria's GDP into off-budget accounts, thereby making two-thirds of government revenue unaccountable.[55] Over decades, a quarter of Nigeria's oil revenue, $50-$100 billion, "disappeared," enabling a corrupt class of politically oriented million-aires.[56] These are sadly recurring events in Nigerian history, and their origin and ramifications deserve examination to better understand Nigeria's broken political economic circumstances.

The more academic term for the curse of natural resources is a "rentier" state, in which an easily con-trolled valuable commodity brings income or "rents," rather than "a return on capital or entrepreneurship . . . [I]t is wealth without work."[57] The dominance of oil exports in Nigeria makes it a rentier state since government revenues are derived mainly from export of state controlled oil.[58] The ability to receive state revenues independent of taxation and the will of the people is a potent force that may expand the jurisdic-tion of the controlling (usually central) government; encourage politicization of minorities and regions over redistribution of rents; eviscerate other economic sectors as already shown; and increase reliance on the "substitution of public spending for statecraft."[59] Wealth without work attracts entrepreneurially tal-ented Nigerians and organizations away from en-hancing the economy through improved agriculture, industry, or services into self-interested public rent seeking activities which misallocate skills and efforts in the overall political economy.[60] Rents are sought for direct wealth derived through corruption and embezzlement, but also for the power and influence they yield when distributed through the political economy to major interest groups in the private sector, ethnic groups, and government.[61] The allure of concentrated oil wealth and power was probably also an underlying motive of the 1967 civil war.[62] The wealth from rents may be dispersed through business contracts, foreign exchange manipulation, appointments to public office, trade controls, and bloated public sector employment among other ways.[63] These rentier state behaviors account for Nigeria's diverted wealth and sapped potential.

Control of state resources is a sure means to wealth and power in a rentier state, and the more avenues to resources, the more the revenues can be tapped.[64] In 1960, Nigeria comprised three large economically viable formal political regions that balanced the power of the federal government. In response to a variety of ethnic, regional, and religious rivalries and to counter the threat of secession, Nigeria sequentially fragmented into 36 states by 1996 (with more proposed but never implemented). This fracturing allowed some form of self-determination and economic control for each majority in the ethnically favored new states.[65] However, it established fault lines that vastly increased the power of the central government, because most smaller states grew to depend on federal handouts as their bureaucracies increased, and it shut out the many smaller minorities not represented as the majority in a state of their own.[66] The federal system in Nigeria has been chronically manipulated, often promoting regional interests over national ones.[67] States from which natural resources originate, mainly in the oil producing Niger Delta region, have gained more revenue through the rent allocation principle of "derivation," which compensates the resource producing states with greater cuts of the derived wealth, now standing at 18 percent of rents compared to just 3 percent in the early-1990s, although still not as much as the producing states desire.[68] In 2004, a third, or \$2 billion, of federal revenue sharing went to four oil producing states, but little of that was used to improve infrastructure and public services.[69] Control over these target states is a lucrative objective of their rent seeking elites, and makes vulnerable the rest of the states, which depend upon the central government's revenue redistribution and subsidies.[70] A stronger centralized government makes rent seeking more attractive and easier to dominate, thus raising the stakes for all involved.

Another downside to the political economy is that those elites in power, enjoying the benefits of rents, tend to hinder general economic growth by concentrating on maintaining the status quo (referred to euphemistically as "sharing the national cake") rather than building development initiatives (making the cake).[71] This maximizes the immediate resources available to the elites in power, since their tenure is often uncertain and panders to short-term distributive pressures from constituents rather than long-term economic investments.[72] Some constituents of elites in power benefit from these arrangements in the short term, but such patronage and poor governance weakens state institutions through less accountability, buying allegiance of some groups through patronage and programs, and alienating opposition groups out of power, since they claim little influence through taxes or voting.[73] The Nigerian armed forces comprise another organization that benefits from the rentier system, since their power (either in controlling the government or threatening to do so) ensures larger spending on the armed forces at the expense of education, health care, and infrastructure.[74] As distribution of government controlled revenues increases, so does conflict among groups and individuals over receiving those distributions.[75] If such ethnic, religious, regional, or organizational representation by its elite is viewed as a Nigerian form of democracy, it is a peculiarly selective representative form that seems to forfeit the general and future welfare of its people.

Nigerian society traditionally depends on client-patron relationships, and many constituents expect leaders to claim control of public resources to benefit their supporting interest groups through bribery, nepotism, extortion, and favoritism.[76] Subordinates are often convinced that they gain when their identity groups benefit from the actions of politicians and are thus mobilized to their service.[77] This allegiance is reinforced when politicians can deliver public goods to their constituents through patronage when the state is ineffectual at doing so.[78] To shore up their positions, Nigerian leaders may demonize rival identity groups to exacerbate their constituents' collective anxiety and mobilize their self-centered support.[79] This explains the Nigerian elite's relentless pursuit of government office through harnessing the antagonisms of their constituent groups to demand representation and access to rents in the form of redistributed public revenue.[80] Unfortunately, the trust of Nigerians in these groups is misplaced since greedy leaders usually leave little to trickle down, as is evident in the destitute Niger Delta states.[81] Elites also tend to be dismissive of their clients except when manipulated in support of the elites' interests.[82] This toxic mixture of motivations leaves the Nigerian polity with weak institutions, exploited subordinates, escalating violence that fractures Nigerian unity, and a poisoned political economy.[83]

In a rentier economy, holding a government office becomes one of the most effective ways of gaining personal riches and power, and it creates elites who mainly look after their own interests.[84] Nigerian leaders have ample opportunity to overtly manipulate the political economy to their advantage through measures such as preventing repairs to government refineries to benefit vested interests in imported petroleum products or stalling construction of much needed power plants to profit from generator sales.[85] Another visible form of rent seeking is in financial services, where liberalized rules in the 1980s allowed authorities to steer opportunities to cronies in banking and the privileged could profit from currency control and foreign exchange schemes.[86] Rent seeking through such overt manipulative methods also encourages illegal transactions such as petroleum diversion, drug trafficking, and commercial fraud.[87] The military elite especially gained from bunkering through exceptional access to oil, resulting in hundreds of millions of dollars of smuggled petroleum, explaining in part the abiding interest in politics by high-ranking military officers.[88] Since 1975, it is estimated that $50-$100 billion of Nigeria's over $400 billion in oil revenues have "disappeared" to corruption and fraud.[89] All of this leads to the practice of "godfatherism," where powerful political financers sponsor elected officials in return for "influence in running of the state, contracts, money, allocation of resources, amenities, employment appointment, etc., in favour of the godfathers."[90] Little wonder, then, that "six of the world's 100 richest men are Nigerian, and each is politically powerful."[91] Nigeria ranks poorly in perception of corruption, with a score of 2.4 out of 10 in 2011, placing it 143rd of 180 countries worldwide.[92] Corruption also explains why the elite resort to crime, including electoral fraud, killing, violence, intimidation, and imprisoning opposition members to protect their own elite positions.[93] On the personal, organizational, and group levels, corrupt policy and institutionalized public crime are demonstrably harmful to the political economy.

Although clearly a detriment, when some forms of extralegal public actions are accepted as regular practices or even encouraged by segments of society, are they still corruption?[94] In Nigeria, a long tradition of client-patron relationships is ingrained in society, where northern elites, for example, have ruled for 200 years through patronage and religious support.[95] Even if these practices are a customary part of Nigerian life, the extreme to which such conduct has gone, in comparison to acceptable international norms, has made Nigeria's elite seem particularly "venal, partisan, [and] self-serving."[96] Despite President Olusegun Obasanjo's declaration of zero tolerance for corruption during his reign from 1999-2007, corruption remained heavy throughout his administration and continues afterwards.[97] However, in reaching compliance in 2011 with the Extractive Industries Transparency Initiative (EITI), the international standard for financial, physical, and process management of natural resources and their revenues, Nigerian politicians have displayed rare political will over a contentious aspect of the problem by implementing a strong governance regime over their resources.[98] That is a good start, but laws without adequate implementation are of little help, as abuse of past parliamentary and presidential type constitutions could not prevent earlier destructive partisanship, corruption, and extreme violence in Nigeria. Even if the Nigerian EITI code should hold, the parochial political fighting over distribution of revenues and its attendant evils will continue. Such revenue is a rich, but finite resource in a poor country. Strong leadership can correct the problems of weak institutions and properly execute well-intentioned laws, but Nigeria has seldom seen such leadership. This is where ethnic, religious, regional, political, and other interest groups complicate the operation of Nigeria's political economy.

THE CAUSES OF CLASHES?

The people of Nigeria are a rich mix of many languages, beliefs, religions, customs, and agricultural and political systems. Such diversity could be a national strength for the country, but these differences are more often accentuated to gain advantage for a group or individual at the expense of the general welfare. This is particularly true in an environment of limited resources and a declining political or economic order in which people tend to band together into ethnic, religious, or other groups to better compete against those not of the same ilk.[99] The politicization of such diversity in Nigeria by its elite "instrumentalizes identity" for their manipulation, and these groups are often organized into "Mafia-like associations" used as "pawns on the chessboard of the political elite."[100] Although control over spoils from the political economy may be the ultimate motivating force for fracturing and violence in Nigeria, the splits occur along many identifiable cultural and regional lines over power and distribution of public resources.[101] Since the mid 1980s, the violence attributed to religious, ethnic, political, and economic factors has increased in Nigeria, with between 12,000 and 18,000 deaths under civilian rule from 1999 to 2009.[102] Mass media perceptions may spotlight cultural grounds for Nigeria's violence, but the actual causes are much more interdependent and complex, as this section shows by examining two major fault lines in Nigeria among religious and ethnic groups.

Conflict between the approximately 50 percent of Nigerians who are Muslim and the 40 percent who are Christian is the most obvious of the religious conflicts in the news, since it is easy to differentiate and demonize others, and "exhortations to violence acquire greater potency once framed in religious terms."[103] As in some other parts of the world, Islamic movements in Nigeria seek political reform to conform with religious beliefs or traditional practices, especially in education.[104] Since first demanded in 1978, these movements have attained full implementation of sharia law in nine northern Nigerian states,[105] but with accompanying widespread protest and violence killing thousands of people and displacing whole communities that remain divided and polarized.[106] During the height of the clashes in February 2000, then President Obasanjo declared the resulting fighting the worst violence since the civil war.[107] In response to imposition of Muslim law and the fear of an agenda to make all of Nigeria an Islamic state, some states in the southeast, most vocally Cross Rivers, have threatened to implement "Christian law."[108] Although violence over sharia's implementation has since declined, it remains a constitutional tension between the right to worship and secular values.[109]

Within Islam, intrareligious tensions abound. Although Muslim Nigerians are predominately Sufi, its adherents within the Qadiriyya and Tijaniyya orders have clashed over economic and political power through much of the 20th century. Both have been vehemently opposed since the 1970s by the native Izala group, a Salafist movement, demanding a more orthodox and public role for Islam against these older political and religious structures.[110] Since the mid-1990s, clashes have increased between Sunni and Shia believers in the north, too.[111] Militant Islamism has fomented violence in Nigeria since the Maitatsine sect unrest of the 1980s. The most recent of these militant threats is the group popularly known as *Boko Haram* (meaning Western education is forbidden, which is indicative of its principles). *Boko Haram* operates in many of the same cities as did the Maitatsine and is the most violent of militant Salafist groups in Nigeria today.[112] It has claimed responsibility for numerous terrorist attacks against Christian and government targets that have killed thousands of people since 2003, including the 2011 bombing of the United Nations (UN) Nigerian headquarters in Abuja and the 2012 vehicle-born suicide attacks against senior military officers attending church at the Nigerian Armed Forces Staff College.[113] Some northern politicians have used this group to advance their agenda, but *Boko Haram* is not controlled by the northern elites and seems to receive training and assistance from outside supporters, possibly including al-Qaeda in the Islamic Maghreb.[114] For decades, religious fighting has been reported as a major cause of violence in Nigeria, and it is indeed a convenient foil for mustering support groups.

On the surface, religious tensions may explain some long-term conflicts like those between Muslim Fulanis and Christian Berom and Tarok in the central Plateau State, in which, for example, Taroks are accused of killing hundreds and burning 72 villages in

2002 and 2003.[115] However, this antagonism is more probably a classic economic conflict between pastoralists and farmers, as suggested by the Catholic archbishop of Abuja,[116] describing tensions as old as the Cain and Abel teaching revered in both religions. Numerous cases of interfaith cooperation do exist throughout Nigeria with, for example, the Yoruba, one of the three largest ethnic groups of Nigeria, split among Muslim, Christian, and animist followers who peacefully coexist in their cities and households.[117] In northern Nigeria, far more cases abound of defused conflicts, interfaith consultation, and emphasis on tolerance and respect from Christian and Muslim leaders than are reported.[118] When manipulated, religious differences can become a divisive political tool, adding legitimacy to efforts pursuing power and economic gain, and it is in this light that such conflicts should be examined.[119]

Mobilizing religious groups has been an important tool in Nigerian politics. Although individual Muslims and Islamic groups are found throughout the country, they are most concentrated and religiously-politically active in the 19 northern predominantly Muslim states. For them, Islamic identity fosters a regional unity and maintains established privileges for the elite, especially through controversial demands for sharia law.[120] The Islamic faith rejects the modern secular Western imperative to separate religious and political activities, and since the 9th century, when Islam first arrived in present Nigeria, it has been extensively used by indigenous rulers to legitimize their rule and organize their lands from the early Kanem-Borno Empire to the 19th century Sokoto caliphate.[121] Conversions from indigenous beliefs to Islam were often heartfelt but could also be forced, with some

21

minorities opposing coercion by instead embracing Christianity, with the later advantage of associating with European systems during British rule.[122] Jihad by the people was also used by the great Uthman dan Fodio in the early-1800s, to fight against the elite who exploited the people of his day and also to go on to establish the Sokoto Caliphate and show how mobilization of the faithful could be an agent of change. That method is still used today by extreme groups like *Boko Haram* and some northern politicians who think they can control it for their own purposes.[123] The rise of *Boko Haram,* and the Maitatsine unrest before it, may lay outside the dynamics of the political economy motivations discussed in this monograph and would greatly complicate the quelling of internal divisions in Nigeria should it gain a real following in the country.

Both Muslim and Christian leaders have politicized their faithful's allegiance to mobilize and give dignity to marginalized constituents, demonize opponents, and gain power since "religion provides a legitimizing framework for violence that would otherwise be considered unacceptable."[124] Religion, then, is a fast, easy way to obtain and manipulate power in Nigeria—fighting over position and power rather than developing and delivering relevant policies and political platforms.[125] Thus, for decades, sectarian violence has become a weapon for economic and political gain, including communal distribution of public resources and religiously oriented legal structures, through such overt uses as religious verses in political songs to burning rival houses of worship.[126] Mobilizing religious movements for political causes often brings a sense of empowerment to the marginalized members of society. This is sometimes done quite easily, given the general dissatisfaction of Nigerians with their circumstances, and is often easier and quicker than seeking to motivate them through policy and programs. This may explain why religious beliefs may seem the cause of violence rather than its tool.[127]

Although communal rivalry over faith issues is a factor in Nigeria's conflicts, religious manipulation to gain political economic advantage is more the root cause of divisiveness.[128] Political parties in Nigeria were often organized around regional religious special interest groups. Northerners, with a common history and a more defined regional religious identity, have been particularly effective at organizing collective action for their region's benefit, which explains why northerners have dominated Nigeria politically through most of its history.[129] The Northern People's Congress (NPC), for example, was the dominant party during Nigeria's formation, and, as part of its persona, invoked the legacy of the northern Nigerian Islamic caliphate to its advantage.[130] The National Party of Nigeria (NPN), despite its name, also covertly manipulated religion in its strategies to win Muslim votes as the northern leaning political party that dominated the Second Republic.[131] Although overtly political religious organizations are now banned, Nigeria-wide Islamic organizations like *Jama'atu Nasril Islam* protect their members' interests, while fostering education and spreading the faith.[132] On the other side, Biafran separatists were quite successful internationally, portraying their cause as a Christian east resisting dominance by an Islamic north during Nigeria's civil war.[133] During the tumultuous years of 1983 to 1998 between the Second and Fourth Republics, political parties were often circumscribed or banned, so mainstream religious organizations filled the political void as they "began to resemble political parties; not only did they make important demands, they also mobilized their members."[134] Thus, political activity by religious groups is deeply rooted in Nigeria, and their rivalries have set an enduring model of how to effectively mobilize for power.

Conflict among the approximately 250 ethnic and cultural groups[135] of Nigeria is another commonly depicted source of friction that, like religion, masks political economic roots.[136] Of these many groups, however, 10 constitute 80 percent of the population, and only three groups — the closely aligned Hausa and Fulani in the north (28 percent), Yoruba (20 percent) in the southwest, and Igbo (17 percent) in the southeast — dominate politics and the economy.[137] As with the NPN and NPC mentioned earlier as examples of parties which used religious affiliations for political purposes, ethnic allegiance was also the basis for forming political parties in Nigeria (and since ethnic and religious identity are often commonly held, there is much overlap in these processes). Also, like religion, allegiance is an easy and efficient means to mobilize support for a political party by saving on recruiting and organizational time and costs, and assuming the cloak of social justice among its members while avoiding substantive policy matters.[138] This practice traces back to the British colonial policy of indirect rule, or Native Authority, under which culturally affiliated power prevailed through the use of existing traditional ethnic elites. Political parties coalesced around these self-interest ethnic groups when such activity was allowed in the 1940s and created an "aggressive regionalism based on cultural, religious, and economic differences," which intensified in the politics of independent Nigeria.[139] Ethnic and cultural affiliation remains a common, if less overt, practice in Nigerian politics today.

Powerful political parties into the 1980s often represented regions and "grew out of ethno-religious and cultural associations" such as the *Egbe Omo Oduduwa* in the Yoruba southwest which became the Action Group; the *Jamiyya Mutanem Arewa* in the Hausa-Fulani north forming the NPC and Northern Elements Progressive Union; and the National Council of Nigerian Citizens formed from an array of cultural associations and labor movements primarily in the Igbo southeast.[140] These arrangements, however, left hundreds of minority groups either dependent upon one of the three major ethnic-regional parties or essentially disenfranchised, and sometimes resulted in defining other ethnic groups as political rivals.[141] Ethnic parties were important in Nigeria because to advance as a community meant controlling government to ensure access to its resources and power. Once in power, the communal group must dominate to prevent the rise of competitors.[142] These rivalries, based upon ethnic, religious, and regional alliances, waged zero-sum fights against each other rather than national political parties addressing strategic issues.[143]

An example of such rivalry comes from one of Nigeria's first political crises, which forced the partition of the Midwest Region from the Western Region in 1963, starting the fragmentation and Balkanization of Nigerian states.[144] At the time, cocoa was Nigeria's major export, primarily a rentier product, and grown mostly in the southwest. An alliance of northern and southeastern interests assured the alliance's federal distribution of cocoa revenues, and was opportunistic in rending the Western Region as a way to weaken the Yoruba monopoly over cocoa production. When oil was discovered in the southeast in 1965, this alliance dissolved and a northern-southwestern alliance formed to ensure distribution of oil revenues.[145] This alliance fought Biafran independence when southeastern interests sought full control over oil (and to counter ethnic violence against Igbos) through secession, leading to a half to two million deaths.[146] From its beginnings, Nigerian politics has been fraught with political-economic ethnic clashes.

The historic momentum of ethnic based clashes still roils Nigerian politics but not as overtly as in its past. Historically, Nigerian political parties were mainly determined by ethnic affiliation and were often hostile to one another.[147] The poisonous effects to the national well-being from tribal and sectarian political organizations was clear after the Nigerian civil war, however, and became the catalyst to ban political parties with ethnic or religious affiliations in the 1979 constitution and again in the 1989 and 1999 constitutions.[148] In addition to the prohibition of ethnic and religious parties, the constitution further stipulates that political parties contending at the national level also have countrywide representation to encourage nationwide support and address national issues. A Nigerian president must not only win a simple majority of all votes cast in the country, but also at least 25 percent of the vote in two-thirds of the states.[149] Within these laws, however, modern Nigerian politics have retained regional, ethnic, and religious biases since political activity was again allowed in 1998. Modern parties often hold a strong base in a region associated with an ethnic group or religion such as the Unity Party of Nigeria and the Alliance for Democracy, both from the southwest, the governing People's Redemption Party from the north, and the All Progressive Grand Alliance in the southeast—many centered around competing elites.[150] Despite the ban on ethnic and religiously based political activity, this long Nigerian tradition of ethnic group advocacy and manipulation continues through ethnically organized violence for parochial political interests and control of resources,[151] but the law itself may play a role in ethnic and religious fighting, also.

Despite laws to the contrary, ethnic and religious affiliations remain an important basis for achieving political demands and redistribution of public wealth in Nigeria. As corruption and weak governance continue, Nigerians have found consolidated ethnic action a better means to meet their expectations.[152] The best example of this is in the Niger Delta region which, although the source of most of Nigeria's oil wealth (producing $200 billion in a decade), endures the lowest standard of living in the republic, suffers under heavy patronage and corruption, and hosts a severely degraded environment from the production of its resources.[153] The 60 or so minority groups living in the delta are mainly disenfranchised and believe they should receive more than the 18 percent of revenue from their oil wealth that the region currently receives under Nigeria's "derivation principle."[154] Not surprisingly, the emerging cultural and political entity, who call themselves the "Delta People," also host Nigeria's most potent, if currently suppressed, independence movement and at least two liberation factions, the Niger Delta People's Volunteer Force and the Movement for Emancipation of the Niger Delta.[155] The "Delta People's" identity is, in part, a tool of Delta politicians who encourage its creation and the violent actions of local groups as means to gain greater share in Nigeria's oil revenue distribution than they had been able to obtain through working within the system.[156]

The general lack of community security and adequate core government services throughout Nigeria has encouraged the rise of vigilantism and ethnic militias to provide protection through organizations such as the Odua Peoples Congress, a nationalist Yoruba group, and the Bakassi Boys, Igbo vigilantes — all of which resort to violent actions to pressure outside groups to attain their political or economic demands.[157] As already shown, the situation in Nigeria is played as a zero-sum game. Ethnic and religious groups feud with each other over scarce Nigerian resources and ideological differences, such that ethnic and religious clashes remain a chronic problem, with over 40 major communal clashes recorded from 1999 to 2002.[158] In a randomly selected recent 2-week period in August 2012, 57 people were killed through ethno-religious clashes and their suppression.[159] In all of 2012, the most deadly year yet, *Boko Haram* is reported to have killed about 770 people through terrorist attacks.[160] Although such groups and activities are illegal in Nigeria, the groups endure because they need to meet their members' needs when the government cannot do so, despite the cost to the general welfare.

The law itself also makes ethnic battles more common in Nigeria as a venue to assert control over the political economy. The concept of "indigeneship" is enshrined in the 1999 constitution as the "'original' inhabitants of a local government area, or members of those ethnic groups that trace their lineage back to the area. All others are considered 'settlers' or migrants."[161] Originally this device was meant to preserve the culture and authority structures of native minorities, but it has become polarizing by excluding some basic rights of nonindigenes in terms of political participation, land ownership, obtaining a job, or attending school.[162] In practice, some citizens have different rights at the local and national levels, which contravene other constitutional guarantees of freedom from discrimination and freedom of movement within the federation—an ambiguous paradox that creates friction and violence in society.[163] These problems arise when an indigenous population fears domination by a migrant group with the diminishment of its own political power and the economic consequences that may result.[164] "Elected officials, in turn, have a strong incentive to issue certificates [of indigeneship] as a tool to consolidate local ethnic majorities," a practice dating back to the 1960s and giving local officials great power. However, this practice also leads to "sharp differences in intergroup inequality, intercommunal animosity, and social fragmentation."[165]

The differences within regions where principle occupations are either agrarian or pastoral, such as the Plateau State, exemplify the problems of indigeneship; though a single political entity, the Plateau encompasses the seams of many religious and ethnic groups and has become the locale of considerable conflict, though it had previously epitomized the slogan "home of peace and tourism."[166] Here indigenous politicians and groups fear and denigrate Muslim migrants (particularly Hausa and Fulani settlers) desiring to dominate local politics like they once did when Plateau was part of the former Northern Region before the 1976 "Christian indigene emancipation."[167] Continuing the example of the agricultural Berom minority, who are bereft of federal patronage or connections, they have experienced the abuse of federal power to take away their lands or pollute them from nearby tin mines, and fear the better connected Hausa and Fulani will further displace them as the latter's powers grow locally.[168] The 2002-03 violence by native Tarok in Wase against Hausa and Fulani villages and the 2004 Tarok bloodshed killing of hundreds of Muslim Jarawa were about "interlopers attempting to claim [indigene] benefits to which they were not entitled."[169] Such desperation stems from "political marginalizations and economic deprivation," compounded by poor governance and opportunistic ethnic leaders.[170] Those labeled as migrants see instead a policy that guarantees an entitlement to local power and resources leading to corruption and partisanship, which contravenes basic civil rights in the constitution.[171] From Plateau State's capital of Jos to the conservative Muslim northern state of Kaduna to the oil-rich southern Delta State, and many places in between, "the material ramifications of losing indigeneship are tangible drivers of [communal and ethnic] violence."[172] Control over political power and economic well-being through the advantages of indigeneship is the central underlying factor upon which religious, ethnic, and regional rivalries, violence, and fragmentation occur.[173]

Even when the law in Nigeria is more straightforward than the confusion over indigeneship, poor governance and implementation also fosters cultural conflict over power. The rule of law remains weak in Nigeria in part because of corrupt and self-serving leaders who have ample opportunity to bend or ignore even the constitution. Section 11 in the 1999 constitution (and similar sections in earlier constitutions) specifically bans formation of any state religion, but that has not stopped full implementation of Islamic sharia law in nine northern states and partial implementation in three more.[174] In another example, the law that ensures wide representation in different ethnic regions of the country in presidential elections was flaunted during the 1979 elections that initiated the short-lived Second Republic. In that election, the required representation of two-thirds of the then 19 states in Nigeria was assumed to round up to 13 states. However, the leading contender, Alhaji Shehu Shagari, received the necessary 25 percent representation in only 12 states. To avoid a run-off election, the Nigerian Supreme Court reinterpreted two-thirds to mean 12 2/3 states, and awarded the presidency to Sharari based on a contrived geographic-mathematic interpretation.[175] These are just two examples of why, "It is often said that it is not good constitutions that Nigeria lacks, but good leadership."[176]

Another constitutional principle, "federal character," is meant to accommodate "diversity, fostering inclusiveness and promoting national unity" in staffing the federal government.[177] Such seemingly beneficial ethnic balancing, however, has led to informal provisions like the zoning system to apportion federal employment.[178] This extralegal arrangement splits Nigeria into six geopolitical zones,[179] and at its highest levels aims to power share the top federal positions among the regional elites on a rotational basis. Although meant to foster harmony, its implementation is neither democratic nor meritocratic, and is already skewed by the election of the "south-south zone" President Goodluck Jonathan in 2011 over expectations (and subsequent violence) by northerners that their region's candidate deserved the nomination of the ruling People's Democratic Party.[180] The good news from these elections is that they were considered the most democratic since 2000, and the election of a minority Ijaw as president holds promise for a more democratic future in Nigeria.[181] A lack of a shared national identity, however, leaves Nigerian politics open to these types of machinations among rival political, economic, cultural, and regional interests.

Given the conditions in Nigeria, cultural and regional fighting over political economic power seems unavoidable. Hostility over scarce but valuable assets, such as patronage and public revenue distributions, "becomes inevitable under conditions that politicize ethnicity and enlist governmental powers in socio-economic competition."[182] Group interest theory expects people with common interests to band together to influence public policy, with each group's strength depending upon its numbers, wealth, organizational strength and leadership, access to power, and internal cohesion — the latter including ethnic or religious affiliations.[183] Cultural groupings seem necessary to maintain or improve economic well-being by those involved, often through the power obtained from politics.[184] This situation inspires the Nigerian euphumism to "get their fair share of the national cake . . . to loot enough resources to dispense to their villages or among their ethnic group."[185] When one group becomes institutionally dominant in a society, the government may lose its ability to cope with societal changes, which may be destabilizing.[186] For much of its history, the Nigerian government and military have been dominated by northerners, leading southerners to push for more "decentralization of the federal government and constitutional changes."[187] Northerners, for their part, fear that liberalization of the Nigerian system will diminish their dominant position in politics.[188] Entrenched positions and competition for limited resources have fostered ethnic and religious conflicts over power and wealth.

Nigeria's diversity along its many cultural and regional lines may seem to be the cause of its problems; however, those differences are often the weapons wielded by elites of the powerful groups for their own gain in political power and economic spoils.[189] Elites from all of the regions not only tolerate the gross inequality their system entails, but also feel entitled to it, despite the greater ensuing harm to social and economic development and political stability in Nigeria.[190] The instrumentalization of identity by Nigerian elites over who receives existing public resources rather than developing those resources further is a failure of good governance and leadership. Thus, deadly fractures occur ethnically, religiously, and regionally that upset stability in Nigeria and may threaten its very unity. While democracy now seems to be taking root and the economy grows, Nigeria's many past cycles of autocracy and stagnant economic growth leave the country brittle and exposed.

NIGERIAN INSTABILITY

Nigeria's importance to U.S. interests stems from its towering political, economic, and demographic influence in Africa, and its rich natural resources and market potential. This is true, however, only while Nigeria remains a functioning integrated state. Thus, the United States, along with the rest of the world, maintains an interest in the viability of Nigeria; as the 2006 Congressional Budget Justification for Foreign Operations notes, "disruption of supply from Nigeria would represent a major blow to the oil security strategy of the U.S."[191] As this monograph has shown, however, Nigeria is under considerable internal pressure over power and spoils through competing regional, religious, and ethnic camps that have racked it with chronic and severe violence to the point of fracturing. Since its independence, the internal political divisions in Nigeria have increased from three to four in 1963, to 12 in 1967 (to unsuccessfully counter the Biafran secession), to 19 in 1976, to 21 in 1987, to 30 in 1991, and to 36 in 1996. A call for an additional 35 states in 1994 was ignored by the framers of the 1999 constitution in an apparent effort to stabilize the situation and halt further fracturing.[192] As many of the past problems that have caused fragmentation continue, mismanagement of a recurring economic downturn or periodic political crisis by the country's elite in the current inflammatory ethnic and religious environment could again result in the need for force to keep the brittle state unified.[193] Although causes for the devolution of the Nigerian state are clearly the power and spoils of the political economy using its ready religious, ethnic, and regional factions, those alone are probably not sufficient for the breakup or failing of the country. Despite its present strains, Nigeria currently remains a functioning and influential state to the extent needed by Nigerian and outside interests.[194] Under what conditions, then, could this balance tip into more dire circumstances? This section analyzes the possibility and gravity of Nigeria's political stability as an incentive to consider this monograph's conclusions and the recommendations that follow.

Parceling a state along cultural divides is an oft-used means to diversify power and reduce minority fears of domination by stronger groups.[195] Despite its good intentions, though, subdividing Nigeria has encouraged the worst in parochial self-serving activities, as unrelenting violence and political machinations show.[196] Splintering is a means to reduce a rival's power when sparring over the political economy, as occurred in 1963 with the forced partition of the Western Region; it was also a means to reduce the strength of the oil-rich Eastern Region during the civil war.[197]

Subdivisions entrench a state's majority group in its local power, but this method may also undermine a dominant group when a minority succeeds in subdividing again to create new majority groups in smaller states.[198] The allure of devolution includes creating new patronage opportunities within ethnic constituencies and controlling wealth distributed by the federal government.[199] Subdividing, however, weakens each of the states with respect to the central government, as smaller, less viable states are essentially obligated to federal officials for revenue and patronage in order to operate.[200] Officials also used the creation of new states as a "diversionary tactic" from the need to address the causes of economic and political problems rather than just their cultural symptoms.[201] One procedural technique tried to counter devolution, but made the situation worse when sharing public revenue from the central government to the states did not ensure fealty to the country. This occurred because the distribution formula gave a fixed amount to each state and an allowance for its population, which became an incentive to create more states, since that would ensure an increased amount of the fixed dividend without reducing the proportional amount received for population.[202] For these reasons, Nigeria has fragmented throughout its history, and recent policies have sought to counter this devolutionary trend.

If internal fragmenting is clearly an existing pressure within the Nigerian polity, what additional forces might push the state to break up? Paul Collier and Anke Hoeffler examined the political economy of secession and found that secessionist communities formed when they perceived an economic advantage to do so. Although such an advantage was not the only way to motivate secession, it was a particularly potent method. An additional economic characteristic enabling secession occurs when the economic advantage, often a lucrative natural resource like oil or cocoa, is spatially concentrated so that an identity group might coalesce around it. Nigeria, with its dependence on oil exports from the southern part of the country, is thus prone to secession,[203] as Biafra (and the still active, if small, Igbo Movement for Actualization of the Sovereign State of Biafra) and the more recent Niger Delta insurgency have shown.[204] The relatively prosperous southwest Yoruba region is a geographically concentrated ethnic group with a natural resource, cocoa, associated with civil conflict and smoldering autonomy and secession movements since the 1990s.[205] Normally, more control over economic resources is only one of several grievances declared for secession, as the Niger Delta Now website shows by also citing greed; disenfranchisement; educational and health inequality; and ethnic, religious, and gender discrimination as grounds for independence.[206] Political control over native economic resources, however, would solve many other existing problems, and thus could be a spur toward partition. Economically richer regions with concentrated ethnic groups, like some of Nigeria's southerners who feel politically dominated by northerners and economically exploited, set the stage for internal divisions to grow into independence.[207]

Concentrated resources may actually create the identity groups necessary to begin a secession movement. The use of terms like tribe, ethnic groups, and nations are amorphous in a society as complex as Nigeria's, and cultural allegiances and designations may shift. During the Nigerian civil war, many southeastern people associated themselves with the Igbo movement to create Biafra, as it was a viable means to regional political independence and increased economic wealth. Most of these same groups annulled their relationship with the Igbo people and renounced the Biafra movement after defeat.[208] Ethnic determination is neither definitive nor static in Nigeria and often based on 19th century European designations of convenience because true Nigerian cultural associations are multifaceted and often indistinct. For example, the concept of a "Delta People" is being developed to bring together over 60 disparate groups in the Niger River Delta region to create their own identity as part of a political process for greater control over economic resources and development prospects.[209]

The opportunity for increased wealth may be more important than past grievances in forming an identity group bent upon secession, especially if the population is uneducated and susceptible to an exaggerated sense of common identity, and the imperative to control localized resources is strong.[210] For example, in Biafra, oil was located along the coast around Port Harcourt and not the inland Igbo cultural core around Enugu, necessitating the creation of a greater Igboland to gain support for secession.[211] Experience with autonomy or previous secessionist ambitions is another factor in secession, and one which may help determine where future Nigerian divisions occur.[212] Thus, convenient ethnic loyalties based around economic advantage are a strong factor in state fracturing, and Nigeria's history indicates that the potential for devolution remains strong.

Should mismanagement of circumstances in Nigeria cause the state to break up, the new states would likely form along lines of past politically autonomous regions.[213] Such regions are often the historic shorthand for traditional divisions reflecting differences in physical geography, agricultural and economic zones, and religious and ethnic peoples that, together, define distinct and internally homogenous areas. So, in addition to the modern construct of a compact economic resource and sense of exploitation around which an identity group may form, a distinct historic contiguous political territory is another trait of secession since it is an easily recognized rallying point for its members. Elsewhere in Africa, similar historic splits are found between Ethiopia and Eritrea, Somalia and Somaliland, and North and South Sudan.[214]

In Nigeria, these splits existed under the early British imperial administration, based on the differences found in older precolonial native states. The 19th century Fulani Sokoto Caliphate and Hausa-dominated remnants of the centuries-old Bornu Empire were first absorbed by British royal charter companies in 1885 and officially annexed as the Protectorate of Northern Nigeria in 1900.[215] Similarly, Nigeria's southwest contained Yoruba-dominated states, including the Kingdoms of Oyo, Benin, and Warri.[216] This area was first ruled by the British when Lagos and surrounding areas were annexed in 1861 to combat the slave trade and formally incorporated as the Colony and Protectorate of Lagos in 1886.[217] True to their cultural heritage, the people of the southeast traditionally governed themselves in decentralized communities, setting them apart from the other regions and making the subsequent indirect rule by the British difficult and inefficient.[218] The British, nonetheless, established a patchwork of protectorates starting in 1849 with the Bight of Biafra, followed by the Bight of Benin, Brass, Bonny, Opobo, Aobh, and Old Calabar. In 1885, these protectorates, stretching from the Niger River eastward to Old Calabar, were assembled into the Oil Rivers Protectorate and re-established as the Niger Coast Protectorate in 1893 and the Protectorate of Southern Nigeria in 1900.[219]

Each of these three regions was administered separately within the British Empire until 1906 when Lagos was incorporated into an enlarged Colony and Protectorate of Southern Nigeria. The Northern and Southern Protectorates joined in 1914, because the North was unable to sustain itself economically and to create the external borders of modern Nigeria.[220] Although adjusted somewhat with time and better understanding of the areas along the internal borders, the lines defining these three key pre-unification areas in Nigeria have remained remarkably durable and significant as relict boundaries within modern Nigeria.[221] Indeed, the north and south continued to be administered separately within the united Colony and Protectorate of Nigeria, and the three regions resurfaced in 1939 when the British created internal political divisions as the Northern, Western, and Eastern Regions, each organized differently for internal self-governing to reflect their separate heritages.[222] In 1954, these regions were reaffirmed under the Lyttleton constitution, which, along with the federal territory in Lagos, became the internal political structure of Nigeria upon independence in 1960.[223] The Biafran secessionists drew upon the legacy of the Eastern Region and its predecessors for legitimacy, as recent Yoruba separatists draw upon the Western Region legacy. Interestingly, Nigeria's most potent secessionist movement today, in the Niger Delta, also has its own legacy bound in part to the Midwestern Region (first of the devolution states in the federal republic), the British Oil Rivers Protectorate, and the native Benin and Warri Kingdoms to create its identity, although that has not been an important element so far in the insurgency.

Despite the delineation of British drawn lines of convenience presented here as enduring internal boundaries, the divides are culturally and geographically less distinct, but the regions' divisions remain potent.[224] The Middle Belt, the southern length of the old Northern Region, including Plateau State, is a transition area of some 180 native ethnic groups partially swayed by northern and southern, Muslim and Christian, and Arab and European influences and is one of Nigeria's most violent regions.[225] The Niger River Delta region is also as indistinct a cultural border, with over 60 disparate ethnic groups, as the river delta itself is an indistinct physical border between Yorubaland and Igboland.[226] Indeed, the delta may constitute a discrete buffer zone through its physical, cultural, economic, and historic identities, real or constructed. Although such intermingling of allegiances and economic interests across Nigeria's internal divides makes secession difficult, violent partitions occurred under similar circumstances between India and Pakistan in 1947 and between the two Sudans in 2011.

Regional, religious, and ethnically inspired violence harnessed by venal leaders has fragmented Nigeria and its people for political and economic gain at the expense of the state. Economically advanced regions in southern Nigeria may be motivated to secede out of the dominating control of the north, using the opportunity offered by their concentrated natural resource advantages. The desire to secede could also fashion the narrative to do so, by creating new coalitions of peoples into an identity group to justify and support separation. Such new identities are especially possible where education levels are low and a history of regional autonomy or previous secession is strong — both conditions found in Nigeria. The danger of the predatory political economy in Nigeria is that it may cause the disintegration of the Nigerian state through enabling these mechanisms. With this very real potential outcome in mind, what can be done to secure Nigeria's long-term unity as a stable functioning state while maintaining U.S. regional interests?

RELEVANT FINDINGS

The essence of this analysis is to explore the main causes of conflict and violence in Nigeria and to explain how those causes relate to one another beyond what is casually understood as common wisdom. In Nigeria, limited or diminishing opportunity and economic disruptions have led to extremely debilitating parochial interests, and they have ignited deadly social and political conflict that is manipulated by corrupt elites.[227] The interactions of the economy, politics, and society are also recognized as fundamental causes of many intrastate conflicts by U.S. *Army Field Manual (FM) 5-0, The Operations Process*, and is certainly borne out in Nigeria. Although such analysis simplifies a very complicated problem in which deeply held religious convictions, fears for ethnic survival, sincere ideological beliefs, societal aspirations, local concerns, population growth, and other human forces play a role, these contributing factors are removed or reduced to a manageable level found in more stable states if the ramifications of a fractured political economy are properly addressed. The emphasis on the political economy as the heart of Nigeria's problems should not diminish these other concerns. It does, however, highlight the core problem to help U.S. Government agencies better concentrate on and address those issues and not their symptoms. To accomplish this, this section will examine some complications in the U.S.-Nigerian relationship, as well as three lessons foreigners need to understand when dealing with Nigerians, and will make some recommendations on how the U.S. military could organize and support Nigerian stability better.

The Design Process, articulated in FM 5-0 and growing in the U.S. military as an important analysis and problem management tool, stresses the crucial importance of examining complex challenges like stability and fracturing in Nigeria. It starts with understanding the conditions around a situation and identifying the right problem as two critical methods that this monoraph has already attempted to do. As FM 5-0 explains the process, it is well-suited for understanding circumstances in Nigeria and how the U.S. Government may approach them better by "examin[ing] the symptoms, the underlying tensions, and the root causes of conflict. . . ."[228] To manage or solve the identified problem, the Design Process next requires that critical thinking be applied to adapt affected processes to a dynamic environment to achieve desired goals. Long-standing U.S. national security goals involving mutual economic advancement, good governance that fairly manages internal divisions, and stable and prosperous regions around the world also apply to Nigeria. With critical thinking in "complex situations that involve political, social, economic, and other factors . . .," the Design Process warns that, "Well intentioned guidance without detailed study may lead to an untenable or counterproductive solution. . . ."[229] Understanding the operational environment, as already presented here, improves decisionmaking and enables integration of the expertise and resources of many U.S. Government, Nigerian, and international assets to best tailor an approach to these problems. FM 5-0 also reminds practitioners that "Design encourages the commander and staff to seek and address complexity before attempting to impose simplicity."[230] With this process in mind, this section will examine the complications that hobble U.S. engagement in Nigeria and why there are only limited steps that the DoD may take in supporting a broader U.S. and international effort to assist Nigerians in managing their own stability and prosperity issues to keep them from becoming larger ones in which the United States must get involved.

Complicating Factors for Outside Support to Nigeria.

The circumstances that created and prolong Nigeria's problems are difficult and complex for Nigerians, but the solution is even more vexing for interested foreign organizations, like the U.S. Government, to influence. With an establishment crippled by structural problems, accumulated past mistakes, poverty, and entrenched distrust, a transforming Nigerian democracy must reform its system and institutions while enlightening an elite and electorate beyond entrenched short-term partisan interests.[231] These problems are compounded in a young democracy by chronic pent up demands and rivalries without the benefit of accepted societal standards of conduct and established institutional procedures.[232] Although non-Nigerians may suggest, influence, and support solutions, every potential improvement must be accepted and primarily implemented by the Nigerians for the sake of legitimacy and efficacy. Nigeria's political economy problems are deeply entrenched and, as mainly internal problems of a proud people, will not lend themselves easily to foreign involvement, especially military influence, for three reasons: Nigeria's insularity, dependence of both sides on oil trade, and the limited expertise of military forces on the fundamental causes of the political economy problems.

Nigeria's regional influence and military power, economic strength, especially in energy exports, and large and diverse population make it one of the key strategic American partners in Africa. Yet, these very characteristics that make Nigeria so important to the United States also insulate it from outside influence or pressures.[233] The decades of steady flow of U.S. aid to Nigeria is an obvious source of American influence; however, such aid simply directs attention to policy issues of American interest, while the Nigerian government's immense source of independent energy revenues and diplomatic stature significantly limit any American leverage through this venue in which the Nigerians are not also interested. The best example of this insularity came during the military dictatorship of President Sani Abacha during the 1990s, a low point in modern Nigerian history, during which U.S. foreign assistance to Nigeria dropped to two token programs, but with little effect on the dictatorial actions of the regime.[234] Nigerian internal rifts also make embracing U.S. agendas or close personal relationships with American leaders anathema, as when President Olusegun Obasanjo was derided by both Sunni and Shia Hausa leaders as "the U.S.'s boy" during political clashes.[235] Indeed, the governments under Presidents Obsanajo, Yar'adua, and Jonathan throughout the 2000s routinely have resisted international assistance for sovereignty and vested interest reasons, which is a situation not likely to change soon.[236] Through 2012, U.S. Government officials found it difficult to even obtain visas for official business in Nigeria, which is symptomatic of the distance maintained in the relationship between the two nations.[237] Any engagement by the U.S. Government to help solve Nigerian problems thus must also be embraced by the Nigerians because it is unlikely to be imposed unilaterally.

Despite Nigeria's political distancing from foreign influence, relations with the United States have generally been pragmatic, in part due to close economic ties. To continue the state distributed energy revenues that all Nigerians support, Nigeria must integrate into the global economy to sell its oil, import food and materials, receive investments and expertise, and conduct its financial business — which leaves some areas for external assistance and influence. Even during the Abacha regime when official contacts were confrontational between the two states, American commercial firms, especially major oil companies, operated normally and even expanded their investments in Nigeria because both sides benefitted.[238] The necessity for Nigeria to export its oil to maintain its domestic status quo, its reliance on a single export commodity, and the fungibility of oil on the world market all suggest points where the two sides may find areas of influence and cooperation.[239] However, maintaining the crucial balance in energy trade, and its associated requirements like investment and relative stability between the two states means that other interests like good governance, democratization, and corruption reduction may languish when both sides do not agree.[240] Thus, although there is some leverage between Nigeria and the United States in the economic realm, any changes that American officials would like to make there will have to be made through persuasion and mutual agreement.

The security arm of the U.S. Government has an even harder role in supporting advancement of U.S. goals in Nigeria. First, given the analysis of this monograph, the Nigerian and international communities should recognize that they do not face security problems as much as economic, political, and social ones; and that any fixes will be mainly in those domains. The role of international defense forces may only be to enable the more fundamental fixes with prerequisite security support or oblique assistance to the other domains. Such support by the military must also be indirect because if the Nigerian government maintains its distance from foreign influence, the Nigerian military is even more nationalistic and independent.

A further complication for foreign military influence in Nigeria is that the root cause of Nigeria's problems, political and economic, are not amenable to the sort of skills that military forces are good at, nor would it be an appropriate example for them to attempt such a mission, short of a military occupation under conditions as found in Iraq or Afghanistan where civil authority no longer functioned. Much of the Nigerian populace would be hostile to direct foreign military influence, since half the population of Nigeria is Muslim. With the worldwide *ummah*'s deep resentment of American actions in Iraq, Afghanistan, Palestine, and other places in the Muslim domain, an American military presence in Nigeria would probably only exacerbate an already bad situation.[241] Thus, although it may be difficult to do, former Secretary of Defense Robert Gates' injunction for the War on Terrorism is equally salient in supporting national stability when he said "the most important military component . . . is not the fighting we do ourselves, but how well we enable and empower our partners to defend and govern their own countries."[242] Thus it may be limited, but U.S. military forces do have a contribution to make to Nigerian stability.

Although the difficulty for foreigners to influence the policies of another state is accepted wisdom, the importance of a stable and unified Nigeria to U.S. interests means the United States must remain engaged and keep as a priority the effort to avert a failed or fractured state resulting from internal tensions that are poorly managed by Nigerian elites.[243] A U.S. Army futures exercise, Unified Quest 2008, explored the possibility of the demise of Nigeria as we know it and found a politically fractured country a distinct possibility. During this exercise, the government of Nigeria failed to adequately recognize it was losing control within its state "to a circle of elites who have seized resources and are trying to perpetuate themselves." Yet U.S. reactions to the situation "were contingent upon what green [the Nigerian government] was willing to tolerate and accommodate."[244] With these caveats concerning the complexities of U.S. influence in Nigeria, this monograph will make some meaningful, if limited, suggestions for U.S. military involvement. These suggestions strive to emphasize gains made by the U.S. military in building upon cultural understanding over the past decade and, in particular, the focusing of aligned units within specific missions to better enable security assistance to meet U.S. interests.

In Nigeria, engagement entails understanding the complexity of its system by foreigners to avoid simplistic or inappropriate responses and to prevent reinforcing counterproductive actions. To address the "wicked problem" that Nigeria represents, and for which the Design Process is well suited, the U.S. Military Academy's Minerva Research Initiative observes,

No longer are military operations won by the most powerful physical force, but rather victory often goes to the smarter, information-dominant, culturally aware, net-centric force.[245]

These observations are not a checklist, but rather are recommended U.S. perspectives and organizational focus that better support the reforms that U.S. and Nigerian government officials determine are needed. Other studies have made many useful substantive recommendations, but the ideas presented here should shape the U.S. military players to better examine and implement these ideas and to handle those that will emerge with time. Through all of this, insight about Nigeria is key, and leveraging that knowledge will produce smarter decisions and a more constructive relationship. This approach will entail bolstering Nigerian institutional development coupled with a balanced engagement that addresses the issues of corruption, conflict, economic growth, and social and economic justice as much as foreigners are able. A more tailored, focused, and cooperative approach may prove to be the most effective method during coming austere times.[246]

Three Lessons Foreigners Need to Understand When Working with Nigerians.

Despite the analysis of this monograph and modern examples of states like the Soviet Union, Yugoslavia, Sudan, and Ethiopia devolving along cultural fractures, readers may find the demise of modern Nigeria sensational. There are certainly pressures on state unity, but unity has prevailed. Indeed, there are considerable centripetal forces, as the next section will show, but centrifugal forces are also strong, and many Nigerians doubt a unified Nigeria really exists.

The first lesson foreigners should know when dealing with Nigeria is that the state's breakup is a real possibility if the Nigerian elite mismanage an acute crisis or one of Nigeria's chronic problems. Abukar Tafawa Balewa, who would become Nigeria's first native Prime Minister, summed up succinctly many Nigerians' doubts concerning their country's indivisibility when, in 1948, he proclaimed, "Many [Nigerians] deceive themselves by thinking that Nigeria is one. . . . This is wrong. I am sorry to say that this presence of unity is artificial." Although Balewa was from the north, members from all of the cultural groups in Nigeria subscribe to such doubts and promote ethnic, religious, regional, or other loyalties over those to the country.[247] The potential for breakup is real because most Nigerians lack "a broad social compact that would establish consensus on national identity and the meaning of citizenship."[248] Without nationally shared values or primary allegiance to their country, Nigerians may be wanting in the constitutional fortitude needed to overcome their many other differences and manage the deep and endemic political and economic problems around which Nigeria is rift. The root of these conflicts can be traced back to the colonial epoch when the new political economy lumped the various people together in a forced new social intercourse. The newly foisted consciousness was readily exploited,[249] resulting in a twisted polity, and, to this day, most Nigerians maintain stronger allegiance to their lineage than to their country. Combine such sentiment with a sequence of political fracturing, a history of civil war, external pressures, and large-scale internal violence, and ignite it with a mismanaged crisis—loose

Nigerian talk of separation could inadvertently lead to fracturing.

The second lesson foreigners need to know is that civil war or the breakup of Nigeria is not inevitable, since few Nigerians want it. That both the state could fail and that few truly want it to is part of the complexity of Nigeria, which must be understood and managed. The fact that both sentiments exist in each of the power groups, from the military to the minorities, is because most everyone benefits from Nigeria's economic unity even while they jockey for a greater share of it through the political economy.[250] Myopic leaders may take their constituents to the brink, but arrangements are inevitably found (with one truly unfortunate exception in the Nigerian civil war) through "key sources of bargaining and accommodation that help to maintain a fragile equilibrium."[251] Such arrangements also date back to the colonial period, and their successes are more common than depicted in the violence-besotted media.[252] In the northern state of violence-prone Kaduna, for example, the Committee on Inter-Religious Harmony is chaired by the governor to identify causes of friction in order to resolve them.[253] Similar organizations calming emotion and promoting harmony are found elsewhere in Nigeria, including the Nigerian Supreme Council for Islamic Affairs and Jama'atu Nasril Islam, which broker peace among various Muslim groups and others. More of such intercommunal dialog will build reconciliation and may resolve the economic, political, and cultural underpinnings that spur violence, and would thus hobble the influence of fringe groups like Boko Haram.[254] As universally appealing as reconciliation may appear, however, this is a form of social justice more in keeping with the Christian doctrine of forgiveness than, for instance, Muslim Hausa "focus on punishment as a deterrent."[255] There are difficulties doing so, but bridging activities at all levels are part of the solution in Nigeria.

In another paradox, a case may be made that there are, indeed, shared values among Nigerians with which to bind them as one nation. One period when Nigerians were more unified and proud came during their economic peak in the 1970s when prosperity was shared, development advanced, Nigeria was widely respected, and its future seemed bright. That this occurred once means that such unity and national purpose could be harnessed again, absent the corruption and poor governance that have felled the country since.[256] Dr. Adiele Afigbo, Nigeria's first great native historian, also finds greater interdependence in precolonial Nigeria through complementary economic, cultural, and historic links among various states and ethnic groups.[257] Forms of cross-cultural interactions existed in terms of "religious, social, and cultural agencies such as age-grade associations, secret societies, marriage ties, and oracle practices," as well as shared ideas and wandering scholars. At the same time, there were divisive influences at work such as interethnic wars and the competition brought about by the slave trade.[258] Thus, Nigeria may have always had coherence although, at times, also internal discord.[259] Building a sense of unity by developing or re-introducing common bonds across Nigerian society is another very important step in maintaining a unified Nigerian state, especially to establish the conditions upon which other solutions are needed.[260] However, shy of becoming a common enemy for Nigerians as the British were during the independence movement, foreigners need to understand this phenomenon, but be judicious in how they support a Nigerian nation concept, lest it be misperceived as something artificial and foisted on the Nigerian people. Resolving the underpinnings of the political economy, while developing a sense of national identity, are sure ways to Nigerian stability, integrity, and progress.

The third lesson for foreigners to understand, as part of their interactions with Nigerians, is that although ineffective or corrupt leadership is a major cause of its problems, Nigeria's institutions have been incapable of curbing abuse of power or ensuring effective and equitable governance.[261] This is, in part, due to many standard Western perspectives and forms not mixing well with Nigerian ways, but the native Nigerian ways have not coalesced well together either.

Nigeria's main regions represent three traditional styles of self-governance. To the north, caliphates and kingdoms used a hierarchical Islamic-sanctioned structure of government.[262] In the southwest, the Yoruba governed through a highly organized set of urban based kingdoms that depended on the rule of local chiefs. The subtribal stage of development of the Sobo, Ibo, and Ibibio groups east of the Niger "[was] where political development had not advanced beyond the clan and family stage [and] where the concept of chieftaincy had made little progress"[263] relying instead on consensual rule. To amalgamate these disparate systems after the 1914 integration of Nigeria, its first Governor-General, Fredrick Lugard, instituted a form of indirect British control[264] through local rulers and structures as "the best way to govern them . . . through the institutions which they themselves had invented."[265]

Although a well-intentioned approach, his inflexible application worked only in the authoritarian north upon which he modeled his ideas and where existed an overlordship system to which the British could relate. Southern systems were less hierarchical, and in the southeast, in particular, no major leaders existed, forcing the British to create such leaders to work through "an inorganic process," to the dismay of its people.[266] By independence in 1960, the British had modified this system to better account for cultural differences by allowing some southern legislators to be elected rather than appointed, and instituting a Regional House of Chiefs as a Western Region government body.[267] Nonetheless, alien colonial rule in Nigeria "twist[ed] indigenous structures and relations until they were ineffective, but [did not replace] them sufficiently with Western substitutes."[268]

Nigerians' native governing systems and the British attempt to govern through them failed, damaging discourse within the political economy. However, unlike the English language, which become the *lingua franca* among its many people, Western governing styles have served modern Nigeria no better.

If colonial rule and forced integration have made indigenous governing schemes dysfunctional in Nigeria,[269] modern attempts at ruling through Western style governance have fared no better. Nigeria has had four different democratic republics, using both British parliamentary and American presidential structures, with dubious performances, although judgment on the current fourth republic must be reserved. Divisive civilian administrations inevitably led to military coups or authoritarian regimes.[270] The historian Afigbo believed that Western governance and economic models did not evolve to address Nigerian political and social conditions and thus remain unsuited for their adopted purposes.[271] One example is the poor results from federalism, where protection, participation, and equality for Nigerian minorities and regions are disregarded by entrenched sectional parochial interests to the detriment of the national good.[272] Another example of the difficulty in applying Western structures is found in the courts of justice, which are often corrupt and backlogged in Nigeria, making local tribal and sharia courts a possible supplement for justice. Customary courts benefit from being more accessible and sensitive to ethnic and religious values, and they may enjoy more legitimacy than formal courts. However, they may also be dominated by local elites and traditional powers and be insensitive to aspirations supporting equality for women and minorities and other modern values.[273] Neither Western nor native governing schemes seem to be a sure route to better governance in modern Nigeria. Thus, part of the complexity of Nigeria is that it seeks to advance along Western economic and political norms to benefit from a globalized environment, but neither its indigenous nor imported forms of government have worked satisfactorily within that environment.

What Nigerians endure are corrupted political and economic systems that have become the battleground for a myriad of self-serving groups, some motivated by religious fervor or ethnic aspirations, but all lacking any real sense of nationalism, seeking to divide revenues from a rich but finite shared natural resource governed by mechanisms ill-suited to the task. Although a daunting indictment, each of these listed issues could be managed and improved by good leadership, the collective lack of which amounts to Nigeria's most grievous failing in terms of internal security as much as political, economic, and social fairness.[274] No matter how perfected the political structure, how rich its economic output, or how dynamic and productive its people, with inadequate or corrupt leadership at the local, state, and federal level, Nigeria will find it difficult to improve its situation.[275]

As this analysis has shown, there are signs of improvement in terms of progress and internal conflict mediation. Perhaps some Nigerian leaders have seen the need to support national interests or have felt some of the pressure from abroad, but these changes may be tenuous. The best way to ensure lasting improvement in Nigeria's condition is by its people no longer tolerating the corrupt, partisan, and violent ways of the past. This would entail making Nigeria's diversity and many institutions work for all, and not just some, which is a tall order for a people so inured to business as it has evolved. To attain stability and prosperity, Nigerians must reform their people's and leaders' concepts of allegiances, share political and economic power and benefits, and work within accepted structures and processes. One piece of that change is in the security sector. Western solutions may not be the best ones for Nigeria, and native solutions should be given leeway, although those are not assured either. There have been many actions proposed for Nigeria by outsiders, and some will probably be helpful, but until the key insights outlined here are understood and used to guide future actions, successful influence may be feeble. To ensure these lessons are better applied in any future actions, some specific recommendations to the U.S. Government, and particularly the military, are offered.

RECOMMENDATIONS: WHAT THE AMERICAN MILITARY CAN DO

It bears repeating that security solutions in Nigeria may be necessary but are not decisive in amending the situation there. To support Nigeria's transition to civilian democratic rule, U.S. foreign assistance climbed from $7 million in 1998 to $109 million in 2001 to $243 million in 2011, displaying a steady growth in engagement that covered areas of mutual interest.[276] These interests emphasized the economic and political domains, which are, at best, indirectly affected by U.S. military efforts.[277] U.S. foreign assistance spending in Nigeria reflects this diminished foreign military role, with an average of less than $2 million per year (only $.5 million in 2011) going to support the Peace and Security category. Nearly three-quarters of total U.S. assistance ($181 million) went to the health sector (with HIV/AIDs [$129 million] and malaria [$15 million]grants dominating), while $32 million went to Democracy, Human Rights, and Governance; $14 million to Economic Development; and $11 million to Education and Social Services.[278] These latter categories address the ingrained political economy problems in Nigeria, but U.S. support has been shrinking because the results from 15 years of investment in political and economic reform have been disappointing. Nigeria's ability to use external assistance effectively seems limited, which is one of the complications of supporting that country.[279] With few U.S. initiatives to support in other fields, security sector assistance to combat Nigerian political economy woes are narrow and often focused on fundamental stability, upon which political and economic reform is based. However, the complications noted of accepting aid and the capacity to use external assistance effectively means more funding is useful only if it enables creative collaborative actions that attack the political economy problem.[280] Nigeria has the financial resources for reform but lacks the will, so it needs American ideas and counsel more than it may need additional U.S. funds.

Even if the direction of U.S. assistance funding does not reflect the importance of political and economic problems in Nigeria, discussions about governance, economics, and security are central to the U.S.-Nigeria Binational Commission—a regular collaborative forum consisting of the highest members of the DoS, Foreign Ministry, and other government agencies, to discuss items of pressing mutual interest. Since 2010, four working groups have covered crucial issues in good governance and transparency, energy and investment, food security and agriculture, and security in the Niger Delta and regional cooperation.[281] Some of these discussions have borne fruit as recent U.S. assistance to the Independent National Electoral Commission supported one of the fairest Nigerian elections held yet, with work starting on the 2015 federal elections and on anti-corruption measures.[282] In the security realm, and indirectly in the others, the U.S. military can assist in improving the situation in some political economy endeavors by sharing operational expertise and can continue to assist in professionalization of the Nigerian military. During austere times, organizations like the Binational Commission, and the partnership between U.S. Africa Command (AFRICOM) and the Nigerian Ministry of Defense, must leverage creative ideas to pursue mutual interests. In operational matters, the U.S. military has experience in internal stability operations in which Nigerians are engaged and in related areas like peace operations, fighting transnational crime, piracy suppression, and counterterrorism. Having engaged in such operations for some time, the Nigerian military will have some things to teach Americans as well.

Internal stability operations and a 2009 amnesty offer to insurgents in the Niger Delta region calmed

Nigeria's worst sectional violence in its oil rich region. Disruptions to oil operations have decreased sharply, and some regular economic activity has returned to normal. Yet long-term solutions to the causes for the unrest are mainly unaddressed, and the U.S. Government and military, with their recent experience in stability operations, may help with this.[283] U.S. Army doctrine and experience includes the interrelated security, economic, political, infrastructure, justice, and well-being aspects of stability operations that would better inform the conduct of the Nigerian government and military.

If such advice and cooperation is accepted, U.S. experts from civil and military agencies could judiciously help the Nigerian government reinvigorate its local, state, and federal capacity in implementing its comprehensive political framework approach toward resolving the conflict in the Niger Delta.[284] In U.S. Army doctrine, such support is part of the security force assistance task in which U.S. forces support, develop, employ, and sustain host nation forces and their legitimate government.[285] However, current U.S. spending and activities with Nigeria have not directly improved stability operations. Since 2008, the request for funds for the Stability Operations subsector[286] of the Peace and Security foreign assistance category constituted about half of the total security aid planned, but has consistently been unfunded.[287] Nigerian military and police forces have not performed well in their internal stability operations, so allowing more U.S. interaction in needed elements of security sector reform would be useful to create the space and time needed for political and economic solutions like President Jonathan's waning initiative in the Niger Delta. However, such interaction is also risky in the domestic politics of both countries, which is why this type of funding and interaction is routinely curtailed.

A partial mitigation to the low stability operations interaction with Nigerian forces is U.S. support for peace operations training funded through the International Military Education and Training (IMET) account. U.S. forces engaged in peace operations support carry less political stigma for domestic audiences in both countries, yet there remains much overlap in the tactical skills, planning, command, training, interagency coordination, and operations found in stability operations activities. This type of training not only supports important Nigerian peace deployments like the U.S. trained battalions in the UN/Africa Union Mission in Darfur (UNAMID) and the UN Mission in Liberia (UNMIL), [288] but should also benefit domestic stability indirectly if these peace operations skills are later used by soldiers employed in the Niger Delta or elsewhere in Nigeria. Training is conducted by the U.S. Government through the Africa Contingencies Operation Training and Assistance (ACOTA) program under Global Peace Operations Initiative (GPOI) funds. Such training is a major source of professionalization for Nigerian forces, which have long had problems with political intervention and human rights violations, and thus is also important in stability operations.[289] In 2011, there were 4,641 soldiers trained through GPOI in 20 courses mostly conducted in Nigeria; in 2012, another 7,043 were trained. Courses were conducted in political-military relations, command and staff operations, prevention of gender based violence, and soldiers' basic peace support skills, among others.[290] These activities certainly reinforce both countries' interests by supporting regional stability, which is their intent, and also support one of only four U.S. policy objectives for Nigerian training assistance.[291] This training benefits stability inside Nigeria by continuing to professionalize the Nigerian military and improve its capacity to conduct necessary stability-like operations, so peace operations support should be offered to the Nigerian government to the fullest extent that it can gainfully be used.

The Nigerian government, with U.S. support, realizes that a comprehensive framework addressing the concerns of the country's parties is needed, particularly in economic development and human welfare services.[292] Within the proposal of stability operations are supporting solutions in the political economy; these are covered under Peace and Security sector aid in the subsector of Conflict Mitigation and Reconciliation, which is used to identify causes of conflict, respond to those causes, and develop lasting solutions "no matter what the cause of conflict might be."[293] This subsector is usually the only one funded—averaging about $1 million per year, although receiving only $.5 million in 2011, and typically only half of what is requested.[294] This small amount with the equally small $.2 million Infrastructure subsector funds in Economic Support sector aid (the account that funds mainly agriculture support) could be seed money to confront the physical and economic poverty that daunts the Niger Delta. Physical economic infrastructure is one striking limitation to economic advancement because of weak government capacity, noted throughout Nigeria, but especially in the challenging geography of the Niger Delta, which has been neglected by the government.[295]

The U.S. Army Corps of Engineers has much expertise in overseeing civilian infrastructure projects in riparian environments that it could offer to assist a comprehensive Nigerian transportation and development plan, especially if international oil giants operating in the region cooperate.[296] Funding for this kind of support could be supplemented by an energized Economic Support Fund, part of the U.S. Foreign Military Assistance Program that promotes "economic and political stability in strategically important regions . . . [for] infrastructure and development projects."[297] This monograph has made the case for Nigeria to be a requisite "special security interest" through which development support should be attained. Infrastructure development is one place where U.S. advice, skills, and some funds can greatly leverage commercial and government actions and build Nigeria's capacity for economic development while contributing to peace and stability.

Another area where both sides may work together to improve internal Nigerian security is in counterterrorism. As with many Nigerian problems, this also has corruption, factionalism, degradation of well-being and economic stagnation as fundamental causes.[298] Unlike the stability operations approach taken by the Nigerian government in the south, Nigeria has used a counterterrorism strategy in the north, especially against *Boko Haram*, but so far has only increased the violence.[299] The United States has not funded Nigeria's Counter-Terrorism subsector of the Peace and Security Assistance fund, despite regular funding requests meant to improve Nigerian capability and institutionalize U.S. strategy.[300] However, the United States does give Nigeria additional security assistance funds through the Trans-Saharan Counter-Terrorism Partnership and the Anti-Terrorism Assistance Program, and has funded training through the Combating Terrorism Fellowship Program, to study regional terrorism issues and intelligence operations, as well as Section 1206, counterterrorism training and support—the latter two usually at less than 5 percent of Nigeria's annual IMET funds.[301] To ensure efficacy in sensitive counterterrorism operations, the U.S. Government has assisted in establishing a counterterrorism unit within the Nigerian military, but support for a similar unit for police forces continues to be barred by Congress.[302] To augment current training, equipping, and organizing, U.S. assistance should also judiciously offer planning, logistical, intelligence, and command and control support to help the Nigerians better use their assistance and hone their operations, reinforcing one of the four U.S. policy objectives for Nigerian training aid, enhancing counterterrorism capabilities.[303]

Several important caveats are needed, however, for counterterrorism and other forms of U.S. security assistance in line with the complications stated earlier. First, direct U.S. intervention, and probably even overt advisor field support, might be counterproductive in the eyes of at least half of the population, the Muslims in particular, and probably many more Nigerians.[304] Second, U.S. counterterrorism support needs to build Nigerian capacity to sustain its own operations and must ensure it is tailored to Nigerian situations, not those of other operations, even successful ones as have been conducted between the United States and Philippine governments. Third, such operations must be planned and conducted within the appropriate confines of Nigerian justice and security to both set the proper example of good governance and to prevent irritating the situation further as current operations have done. In this regard, more advice and training could be offered, especially in regards to police support, and tied to incentives to improve performance along more effective counterterrorism methods to curb abuses and corruption within the system. How much additional assistance the Nigerians may accept remains open to question.

Other areas of cooperation in stability operations, anti-piracy, and transnational crime parallel the causes and solutions outlined for counterterrorism, but should emphasize the law enforcement aspect even more. Transnational crime, trafficking in drugs and humans, and financial fraud are each rampant in Nigeria and debase civil society. However, illegal firearms trafficking is especially threatening to internal security for a land as violent as Nigeria.[305] Better policing and methods would help alleviate all of these problems, and the U.S. Government can supply expertise here.

U.S. military forces could help with improved international border control, through which much of this trafficking is conducted across porous borders that both supply Nigerians and serve as a waypoint to more lucrative foreign markets.[306] Typically only $.1-.2 million in the Transnational Crime subsector of Peace and Security is given in aid to Nigeria, and none has been planned since 2011, although training and technical assistance are this subsector's goals.[307] Instead, the United States has directed millions to fight transnational crime in Nigeria through the International Narcotics Control and Law Enforcement (INCLE) program. Here again, the United States should use what leverage it gains from such assistance to help the Nigerian government in its own efforts to modernize and recruit less corruptible security forces, especially in the police.[308] INCLE also includes the mission of elimination of nacro-terrorism, which complements other potential areas of U.S.-Nigerian cooperation.[309] Lessons gained from Iraq, Afghanistan, and U.S. border operations should help inform the capabilities and limits of military forces in these roles, and offer best ways to supplement Nigerian police forces in better performing their mission.

Piracy around Nigeria is another growing transnational crime. Incidents in the region have grown from 40 in 2008 to 64 in 2011, costing billions of dollars in theft and lost government revenues, and impinging on U.S. imports from a major supplier. This explains why the U.S. training policy goal of "Build and enhance maritime security capacity to maintain territorial integrity and secure uncontrolled waters" is one of four established for Nigeria.[310] The biggest spurs for piracy in the Gulf of Guinea are the impunity of criminal gangs, ethnic militias from Nigeria, and low government capacity to combat it, all factors addressed herein. The United States has supported Nigeria in this fight with material aid, such as the four surplus U.S. Coast Guard *Balsam*-class patrol ships given in 2003. Training support comes through the Africa Partnership Station program, which trains Nigerians aboard transiting U.S. ships in important skills like maritime interdiction operations and counterterrorism.[311] The successes of these programs are a model for additional U.S. aid to Nigeria.

First, they are focused on expertise that U.S. military forces have obtained through actual operations elsewhere in the world and offered as part of regular security assistance. Second, training is conducted directly between military forces where it is needed, but avoids a long-term U.S. presence in country, and it emphasizes an indirect approach of training, rather than conducting operations. Third, transferred property, training, and exercise activities build interoperable capability, which shall be required should an international task force to combat piracy in the region come to fruition, a UN initiative that the United States quietly supports.[312] The anti-piracy program is a mutually beneficial program that supports both sides' expectations and part of the greater effort toward stability in Nigeria's political economy.

To make U.S.-Nigerian military contacts more operationally effective and financially efficient, a DoD-wide program to assign regionally aligned forces oriented to Nigeria, or at least West Africa, under AFRICOM integration should be improved to better implement security assistance and build regional expertise under the direction of the DoS. Regionally aligned forces entail specific units assigned in military-to-military partnerships that delve deeply into local cultures and languages, geography, forces, and challenges.[313] U.S. units and individuals gain insight and establish enduring personal relations through training-focused visits in the equivalent of platoon- to battalion-sized units.[314]

This approach makes sense if one believes there will be no U.S. peer rival for a significant amount of time, during which shaping activities dominate, and U.S. units can engage in security force assistance and support local stability operations.[315] It also makes sense if the DoD parcels high end threats like anti-access/area denial to the Air Force and Navy, while addressing low end threats "by building the military capability of partner nations" through the Army, Marine Corps, and Special Operations Forces as proposed by former Deputy Secretary of Defense for Policy Michele Flournoy.[316] This partnering arrangement allows units to augment training, equipping, and organizing of Nigerian forces, especially in fields requiring understanding of local issues like logistics, intelligence, and command and control.[317] For U.S. Army forces, on whom the brunt of regional specialization would fall, this alignment concept follows the vision imperative in the Army Chief of Staff's *2012 Army Strategic Planning Guidance:* "Provide modernized and ready, tailored land force capabilities to meet Combatant Commanders' requirements across the range of military operations."[318] The benefits of regionally aligned forces include more effective interactions and support, and improved U.S. understanding and interoperability during contingencies and multinational actions in the future.

Elements of this regionally aligned force proposal exist in the DoD, as Special Operations, Marine Corps, and National Guard units are already aligned to Africa, with the Army adding its active duty conventional forces as well. Special Forces units, whose focus is operating in the "human domain" of war, have long specialized in building their competence in the world's regions as advisors and operators to better complete missions like foreign internal defense. The 3rd Special Forces Group at Fort Bragg, NC, currently operates under Special Operations Command Africa. U.S. Army civil affairs (CA) units are also specializing to provide civil-military expertise to conventional forces during theater engagement and full spectrum military operations. Both the active duty 91st CA Battalion (CAB) at Fort Bragg, and the Army Reserve 82nd CAB at Fort Stewart, GA, (which offers more continuity and unique civilian skills than the active 91st), also align with AFRICOM.[319] In 2007, the Marine Corps Training and Advisory Group was commissioned to advise U.S. units and partner nations on security training and organization. Although originally meant to support operations in Iraq and Afghanistan, a special task

force now rotates through Africa on security cooperation missions.[320] Since 2006, the California National
Guard has partnered with the Nigerian military in a
long-term relationship in which the personnel stability inherent in Guard units is particularly effective at
achieving high levels of trust and understanding.[321]
The active duty Army is following the National Guard
in aligning "scalable, tailorable forces" to regions with
the 2nd Brigade Combat Team, Fort Riley, KS, slated
to provide "security cooperation and partnership
building missions in Africa"; this is the first region to
test this rotational model.[322] These alignments, however, are all service component initiatives that should be
harnessed under DoD-wide oversight that specifically
seeks out other units and skills needed in the region.
Together, these dedicated units should offer useful
supplements "in what is essentially a domestic peacekeeping operation" in support of Nigerian stability.[323]

These alignment efforts could significantly augment customized support available to the Nigerian
government. However, such increase does come with
problems and challenges. The first is to get the Nigerian government to accept more of the needed type of
support offered by U.S. defense forces. Second, initial
and continuing education in the region and in specific
mission tasks are expensive and challenging with so
many people involved. Such training will probably
never meet the level needed, but would result in a
greater level of expertise than currently exists. The
investment in trained personnel and established relationships would have to be protected, too, requiring
changes in the personnel system to retain immersed
military members and minimize out-of-unit assign-
ments — in essence creating a regimental system in the
regionally aligned active forces.[324]

In addition to specializing people, unit equipment sets should also be tailored since the configuration that might work in the mountains of Ethiopia or the temperate *veldt* of South Africa might not suit the mission requirements for Nigeria.[325] Functionally-specialized units in the medical, police, and construction fields for example, would be in high demand, meaning they probably could not regionally align but would rely on the expertise of aligned units to shepherd their efforts. Such specialization of U.S. military units works against the traditional flexibility sought by standardizing unit skills and equipment which makes them interchangeable across theaters in large unit operations when contingencies so require.[326] In a major operation elsewhere requiring use of AFRICOM aligned units, all of this specialization will be for naught, as equipment may be mismatched and necessary combined-arms maneuver skills not as strong as their more used stability operations skills.[327] Finally, Africa is a huge region with remarkable diversity in geography, climate, cultures, economies, history, and politics. To have a unit regionally specialize in all of Africa is an errand fraught with problems, i.e., high priority subregions and crucial countries need to be identified and units aligned there, rather than spread thin (although one unit could focus on the noncritical remainder). This monograph has made the case that Nigeria should be one of the alignment focal points in the world.

While this training, exercising, and indirect support is enhancing Nigerian technical capabilities, the military-to-military contacts that are occurring at the same time should also continue to professionalize the Nigerian military and make it a more principled force with better democratic civil-military relations and less corrupt and politicized members.[328] This goal aligns with the fourth U.S. training objective for Nigeria: "Develop capacity of the military as a nonpolitical, professional force respectful of human rights."[329] In fact, the U.S.-Nigeria Binational Commission recognized that extralegal activity by the Nigerian security forces leads to violence and recommended "cooperative efforts to improve Nigerian military and police units."[330] At the tactical level, this means "better intelligence and prevention measures [that avoid a] heavy-handed response," a problem which U.S. training and interactions can address.[331]

At all levels, true respect for civil rights and rule of law is also needed to build legitimacy for government efforts and prevent the spiral of retribution with its citizens. Endemic corruption in the military, from the petty in the ranks to the massive bunkering among flag officers, and a historic propensity to overthrow government administrations must also be curbed for the military to exert a positive influence on activities in the political economy.[332] Here, the example of U.S. military personnel in close partnership over time could influence the Nigerian military to move into a more professional, apolitical stance. More directly, IMET courses at the mid to senior officer level have contributed to the professionalization of Nigerian forces since security assistance was reopened to Nigeria in 2000, and the State Department's Foreign Military Training Report attributes the Nigerian military leadership's proper conduct during recent elections to this influence. [333] Corruption remains a huge problem within the ranks, and although American military relationships and education may reduce this problem, better pay and a change in political attitudes and cultural mores will be needed to fully professionalize the Nigerian forces—changes that are out of reach of direct U.S. military influence. Much needs to be done to improve the civil-military relationship within Nigeria, and U.S. efforts so far are helping, but here more funding for education and exchanges could go a long way.

Support to wide ranging stability operations in Nigeria, including counterterrorism, suppression of transnational crime and piracy, as well as related peace operations, are limited, but are nonetheless useful contributions by the U.S. military and other agencies toward stabilizing and developing Nigeria. A few opportunities to contribute directly to resolving political and economic problems, like infrastructure development and fighting piracy, are available but require funding and partnership at a level the U.S. and Nigerian governments have so far been reluctant to achieve. To get the most from what is available, these and other cooperative actions that are acceptable to both sides, within the restraints of a complicated relationship, are developed in the Nigerian government's Internal Defense and Development (IDAD) plan. This plan seeks to integrate the political, economic, social, and military needs of its government. Elements of the Nigerian IDAD may then be communicated through the Binational Commission to be incorporated by the U.S. Ambassador's country team to harness the considerable capability that already exists within the U.S. Government in order to keep the process streamlined and limit manpower requirements. From this plan, AFRICOM's Theater Security Cooperation Plan (TSCP) would coordinate the tasks and participation appropriate for U.S. military agencies and units, especially leveraging the continuity of regionally aligned forces.[334] A comprehensive IDAD also benefits Nigeria through the synergy that other countries and international institutions may contribute to achieve a cumulative result that no single contributor could afford, but from which all benefit through the stabilization of Nigeria.[335]

CONCLUSION

Nigeria is an extraordinarily important country for U.S. foreign relations in terms of bilateral economic interests, great influence in Africa, and the many mutual interests both countries have maintained through a generally good working relationship. The U.S. Government, therefore, has a particular interest in helping Nigerians overcome the political economic problems that severely divide it internally and threaten its very integrity as a functioning state. That these problems revolve around the divisive use of political, ethnic, religious, and regional groups — in which each tries to improve its position in power and economic revenue at the expense of the other — is why this monograph identified political economic problems as the source of much of Nigeria's instability. Those sources, not the more easily reported symptoms, must be directly addressed if there is to be a lasting positive impact on the recurring crises in Nigeria. Nigeria's chronically poorly performing economy puts pressure on various power groups to obtain their share of its rich public natural resource revenues to benefit their leaders and interest group supporters. Venal leadership and poor government organization and laws often prevent addressing these problems effectively, although attempts by administrations in the Fourth Republic to do better are still being tested.

Nigerians have defined themselves through their differences and not their similarities, which exacerbates the conflict over resources through violence and calls for self-determination that weakens the state.

In many ways, oil production in Nigeria has become more a cause of serious problems than the means to improving the economy and well-being of its people. Nigeria has been poorly governed and is subject to severe corruption that has left its polity divided with fighting over power and revenues rather than enhancing the economy to benefit everyone, a classic example of a rentier state under the "curse of oil." Sectarian and communal groups have been guided by their leaders, often through traditional client-patron relationships, to believe that such divisions are a sure way to improving their situation, and this perspective has been ingrained into the national dialogue. Although religious, ethnic, and regional differences are often how dissension and violence are "instrumentalized" in Nigeria, they should not be confused with the deeper causes of competition over power and resources among a self-serving elite. Despite the best of intentions, the law is contorted in this battle over power through such principles as indigeneship, federal character, derivation, and zoning, which exposes even further the shallowness of leadership in pursuit of "the national cake." Such differences are dangerous to the stability and unity of Nigeria, since the country contains traits found in other secession prone states, and its people are easily divided along recognizable fault lines with the motivation to secede.

Although an important state for U.S. international interests, the United States is limited in what it can do to help Nigeria address its core problems. The relationship is complicated by Nigeria's insular nature; the mutual dependence on oil trade, which limits actions in other fields; and, by the U.S. military's lack of appropriate expertise in the most important problem areas. Where there are areas of cooperation and influence, foreigner members must be sensitive to the fact that Nigeria remains a fragile state, although few Nigerians would have it disintegrate if avoidable. Foreigners must also confront the problem of weak and corrupt leadership that characterizes Nigeria and its relatively weak governing structures that are unable to compensate for the weak leadership.

Within these limitations, the U.S. military must play the hand it is dealt and can best do so through its own strengths in sharing expertise with the Nigerian military in the missions of stability operations, peace operations, counterterrorism, and the suppression of transnational crime and piracy. All of these can also enhance the professionalization of the Nigerian military through regular contacts in exercises and training. Professionalization works best through regular and established contacts, and the alignment of U.S. forces to the region is a trend in the right direction, but more emphasis to get the most out of existing programs is needed. All of this comes with caveats, complications, and costs that are necessary to support a truly crucial partner to American interests.

The recommendations herein recognize that most uses of the U.S. or Nigerian military in addressing the core political economy problems of the country beyond basic security will probably to be indirect at best, and may be an inefficient or inappropriate tool.[336] Police, civilian government agencies, and international and nongovernmental organizations may provide better support to accomplish the necessary tasks and goals for Nigerian stability and progress. However, until the other Nigerian and foreign organizations are funded, focused on political economy solutions, and enabled to plan and execute remedial actions, the current and proposed military options in this monograph, as caveated, are needed to leverage time and existing efforts, and so should be continued where appropriate and coordinated for both synergy and cost savings. During the Binational Conference in 2009, Nigerian Defense Minister Godwin Abbe indicated that cordial standing relations would allow specific U.S. actions to bring peace and security to the Niger Delta.[337] A strong security assistance program to Nigeria could be part of a larger effort at political, economic, and social development designed to address the problems in Nigeria and to help stabilize it, keep it whole, and lead it toward its potential as an influential and prosperous state—meeting both U.S. and Nigerian interests.

BIBLIOGRAPHY

Abdullahi, Salisu A. "Ethnicity and Ethnic Relations in Nigeria: The Case of Religious Conflict in Kano" in Judy Carter, George Irani, and Vamik D. Volkan, eds., *Regional and Ethnic Conflicts: Perspectives from the Front Lines*. Upper Saddle River, NJ: Pearson Prentice Hall, 2009, pp. 292-299.

Adebajo, Adekeye. *The Curse of Berlin: Africa after the Cold War*. New York: Columbia University Press, 2010.

Africa Center for Strategic Studies (ACSS). *2012 Workshop on Security Sector Reform/Transformation in West Africa*. Washington DC: ACSS, October 19, 2012.

Albert, Isaac O. "The Sociocultural Politics of Ethnic and Religious Conflicts" in Ernest E. Uwaizie, Isaac O. Albert, and Godfrey N. Uzoigwe, eds., *Inter-Ethnic and Religious Conflict Resolution in Nigeria*. Lanham, MD: Lexington Books, 1999, pp. 70-87.

Alozieuwa, Simeon H. O. "Beyond the Ethno-Religious Theory of the Jos Conflict." *Africa Peace and Conflict Journal*, Vol. 3, No. 2, 2010, pp. 18-31. Available from *www.humansecuritygateway.com/documents/APCJ_Vol3No2Dec2010.pdf*.

American School of International Service (ASIS). "The Biafran War." Washington DC: American University School of International Service, November 1997. Available from *www1.american.edu/ted/ice/biafra.htm*.

Amoda, John. "Nigeria-U.S. Bi-National Commission and Nigeria Security Interests." *AllAfrica*, October 15, 2012. Available from *allafrica.com/stories/201210160458.html*.

Asuni, Judith Burdin. *Special Report: Blood Oil in the Niger Delta*. Washington DC: United States Institute of Peace, August 2009.

Atoh, Samuel Aryeetey. "Africa South of the Sahara" in Douglas S. Johnson, Viola Haarmann, Merrill L. Johnson, and David L. Clawson, eds., *World Regional Geography*. Upper Saddle Brook, NJ: Pearson Prentice Hall, 2010, pp. 400-465.

Ayodele, Bonnie. "Silence on Climate Change and Natural Resources Conflict in Nigeria: The Niger Delta Region Experience" in Donald Anthony Mwiturubani and Jo-Ansie van Wyk, eds., *Climate Change and Natural Resources Conflicts in Africa*, Pretoria, South Africa: Institute for Security Studies, 2010, pp. 105-122. Available from *www.iss.co.za/uploads/Mono170.pdf*.

Baldauf, Scott. "Next Pirate Hot Spot: the Gulf of Guinea." *The Christian Science Monitor*, February 28, 2012. Available from *www.csmonitor.com/World/Africa/2012/0228/Next-pirate-hot-spot-the-Gulf-of-Guinea*.

Benedict, Akpomuvie Orhioghene. "Breaking Barriers to Transformation of the Niger Delta Region of Nigeria: A Human Development Paradigm." *Journal of Sustainable Development*, Vol. 4, No. 3, June 2011, pp. 210-221.

Berry, LaVerle. "The Society and Its Environment," in *Algeria, A Country Study*. Washington DC: Department of the Army, 1985.

Bevan, David, Paul Collier, and Jan Willem Gunning. *The Political Economy of Poverty, Equity, and Growth: Nigeria and Indonesia*. Oxford, UK: Oxford University Press, 1999.

Blessing, Michael A. *Nigeria's Center(s) of Gravity; A Complex and Violent Operational Environment*. Carlisle, PA: U.S. Army War College, 2008. Available from *www.dtic.mil/cgi-bin/GetTRDoc?AD =ADA478387&Location=U2&doc=GetTRDoc.pdf*.

Bouchat, Clarence. "The North-South Divide within Mediterranean Countries." *Mediterranean Quarterly*, Vol. 5, No. 1, Fall 1994, pp. 125-141.

Bradley, Matthew Todd. "Inter-Ethnic Antagonism in Post-Colonial Nigeria: Ethnicity vs. Symbolic Nationalism." *Journal of Cultural Studies*, Vol. 7, No. 1, 2006, pp. 61-75.

Butty, James. "Nigerian Professor Says Latest Jos Violence a Result of Many Factors." *VOANews.com*, January 18, 2010. Available from *www.voanews.com/content/butty-nigeria-violence-analysis-20jan10-82131892/152914.html*.

Cahoon, Ben. "World Statesman — Nigeria." 2000. Available from *www.worldstatesmen.org/Nigeria.htm#Northern-Nigeria*.

Casey, Conerly. "Mediated Hostility, Generation, and Victimhood in Northern Nigeria" in Judy Carter, George Irani, and Vamik D. Volkan, eds., *Regional and Ethnic Conflicts: Perspectives from the Front Lines*. Upper Saddle River, NJ: Pearson Prentice Hall, 2009, pp. 274-291.

Central Intelligence Agency (CIA). *The 2012 World Factbook*. 2012, Nigeria. Available from *www.cia.gov/library/publications/the-world-factbook/geos/ni.html*.

Cohen, Herman J. "Africa: A Light at the End of the Tunnel?" *Air and Space Power Journal–Africa and Francophonie*, Vol. 1, No. 3, Fall 2010, pp. 6-15. Available from *www.academyofdiplomacy.org/publications/article_archive/Africa%20by%20Cohen.pdf*.

Collier, Paul and Anke Hoeffler. *The Political Economy of Secession*. Washington DC: World Bank Development Research Group, 2006.

Collier, Paul and Nicholas Sambanis. "Understanding Civil War: A New Agenda." *Journal of Conflict Resolution*, Vol. 46, No. 1, February 2002, pp. 3–12.

Concerned African Scholars Organization. "U.S. Military Involvement in Nigeria." African Security Research Project, September 2009. Available from *concernedafricascholars.org/african-security-research-project/?p=83*.

Cox, Dan. "An Enhanced Plan for Regionally Aligning Brigades Using Human Terrain Systems." *Small Wars Journal*, June 14, 2012. Available from *smallwarsjournal.com/jrnl/art/an-enhanced-plan-for-regionally-aligning-brigades-using-human-terrain-systems*.

Crighton, Elizabeth and Martha Abele MacIver. "The Evolution of Protracted Ethnic Conflict." *Comparative Politics*, Vol. 23, January 1991, pp. 127-142.

Cutter, Charles H. *Africa 2007*. Harpers Ferry, WV: Stryker-Post Publications, 2007.

Defense Institute of Security Assistance Management. *The Management of Security Assistance*. Wright Patterson Air Force Base (AFB), OH: DISAM, 2007. Available from *www.disam.dsca.mil/documents/greenbook/v31/01_Chapter.pdf*.

Defense Security Cooperation Agency (DSCA). Fiscal Year 2013 Budget Estimates. Washington DC: DSCA, February 2012. Available from *comptroller.defense.gov/defbudget/fy2013/budget_justification/pdfs/01_Operation_and_Maintenance/O_M_VOL_1_PARTS/O_M_VOL_1_BASE_PARTS/DSCA_OP-5.pdf*.

Dempsey, Thomas. "The Transformation of African Militaries," in Amy Krakowka and Laurel Hummel, eds., *Understanding Africa: A Geographic Approach*, West Point, NY: United States Military Academy, 2009, pp. 387-391.

Department of Defense and Department of State. *Foreign Military Training and DOD Engagement Activities of Interest, 2009-10*. Washington DC: U.S. Department of Defense and Department of State, 2010. Available from *www.state.gov/t/pm/rls/rpt/fmtrpt/*.

Department of Defense and Department of State. *Foreign Military Training and DOD Engagement Activities of Interest, 2011-12*. Washington DC: U.S. Department of Defense and Department of State, 2012. Available from *www.state.gov/t/pm/rls/rpt/fmtrpt/*.

Department of State. "Nigeria." *Background Notes*. Washington DC: U.S. Department of State, Bureau of African Affairs, November 20, 2012. Available from *www.state.gov/r/pa/ei/bgn/2836.htm*.

Department of State. *U.S.-Nigeria Binational Commission Niger Delta and Security Cooperation Working Group Meeting on September 13-14*. Washington DC: U.S. Department of State, Office of the Spokesman, September 2010. Available from *www.state.gov/r/pa/prs/ps/2010/09/147023.htm*.

Department of State. *U.S.-Nigeria Binational Commission Meets Regularly*. Washington DC: U.S. Department of State, Office of the

Spokesman, November 2012. Available from *www.state.gov/p/af/ci/ni/139598.htm*.

Department of the Army. "MAVINI Information Sheet." Washington DC: U.S. Department of the Army, Office of the Assistant Secretary for Manpower and Reserve Affairs, undated. Available from *www.goarmy.com/content/dam/goarmy/downloaded_assets/mavni/mavni-language.pdf*.

Department of the Army. *Field Manual (FM) 3-07.1, Security Force Assistance.* Washington DC: U.S. Department of the Army, May 2009. Available from *usacac.army.mil/cac2/Repository/FM3071.pdf*.

Department of the Army. *Field Manual (FM) 5-0, The Operations Process.* Washington DC: U.S. Department of the Army, March 2010.

Dilegge, Dave. "USMC Forms MCTAG." *Small Wars Journal,* November 19, 2007. Available from *smallwarsjournal.com/blog/usmc-forms-mctag*.

"Dutch Disease." *Investopedia.* Available from *www.investopedia.com/terms/d/dutchdisease.asp#ixzz253jLCVuk*.

"Economic and Trade Overview." *2007 Comprehensive Report on U.S. Trade and Investment Policy Toward Sub-Saharan Africa and Implementation of the African Growth and Opportunity Act.* Office of the United States Trade Representative, U.S. Department of State, May 2007, pp. 21-36.

Ekanola, Adebola. "National Integration and the Survival of Nigeria in the 21st Century." *The Journal of Social, Political, and Economic Studies,* Vol. 31, Fall 2006, pp. 279-293.

Ellis, Stephen. "The Roots of African Corruption." *Current History,* Vol. 105, No. 691, May 2006, pp. 202-213.

Elu, Juliet. "Human Development in Sub-Sahara Africa: Analysis and Prospects for the Future." *Journal of Third World Studies,* Vol. 17, No. 2, Fall 2000, pp. 53-71.

Energy Information Administration (EIA). "Nigeria." Washington DC: U.S. Department of Energy, Energy Information Administration, August 2011. Available from *www.eia.gov/countries/cab.cfm?fips=NI*.

Falola, Toyin. *Culture and Customs of Nigeria*. Westport, CT: Greenwood Press, 2001.

Falola, Toyin. *The History of Nigeria*. Westport, CT: Greenwood Press, 1999.

Falola, Toyin and Matthew M. Heaton. "The Works of A. E. Afigbo on Nigeria: An Historigraphical Essay." *History in Africa*, Vol. 33, 2006, pp. 155-178. Available from *muse.jhu.edu/journals/hia/summary/v033/33.1falola.html*.

Friedman, George. "Financial Markets, Politics, and the New Reality." *Stratfor*, August 7, 2012. Available from *www.stratfor.com/weekly/financial-markets-politics-and-new-reality?utm_source=freelist-f&utm_medium=email&utm_campaign=20120807&utm_term=gweekly&utm_content=readmore&elq=190331b653e84cbb9fd56af99a9be15a*.

Friedman, Thomas L. *The World is Flat: A Brief History of the Twenty-first Century*. Basking Ridge, NJ: Farrar, Straus and Giroux, 2005.

Ghebadi, Victor-Yves. "CSSM - A Chance for Peace in the Middle East." *International Defense Review*, February 1992, pp. 111-119.

Gordon, April A. and Donald L. Gordon. "Trends and Prospects" in Gordon and Gordon, eds., *Understanding Contemporary Africa*, Boulder, CO: Lynne Reinner Publishers, 2007.

Griffin, Steve. "Regionally-Aligned Brigades: There's More to This Plan Than Meets the Eye." *Small Wars Journal*, September 19, 2012. Available from *smallwarsjournal.com/jrnl/art/regionally-aligned-brigades-theres-more-to-this-plan-than-meets-the-eye*.

Hewitt, Christopher and Tom Cheetham. *Encyclopedia of Modern Separatist Movements*. Santa Barbara, CA: ABC-CLIO, 2000.

Igbuzor, Otive. "Nigeria's Experience in Managing the Challenges of Ethnic and Religious Diversity through Constitutional Provisions." Ethnic Nationalities Council, 2012. Available from *www.encburma.net/index.php/feature/54-feature/166-nigerias-experience-in-managing-the-challenges-of-ethnic-a-religious-diversity-through-constitutional-provisions.html*.

Ikpeze, N. I., C. C. Soludo, and N. N. Elekwa. "Nigeria: The Political Economy of the Policy Process, Policy Choice, and Implementation" in Charles Chukwuma Soludo, Michael Osita Ogbu, and Ha-Joon Chang, eds., *The Politics of Trade and Industrial Policy in Africa: Forced Consensus?* Trenton, NJ: Africa World Press, 2004, pp. 341-364.

Imoh, Maurice Iroulor. *The Development of an Atlas of the Nigerian Political Evolution*. Masters Degree Thesis, Columbus, Ohio: The Ohio State University, 1977.

Institute for Security Studies (ISS) Seminar Report. *South Sudan's Referendum – Geopolitical and Geostrategic Implications*. New Muckleneuk, South Africa: Institute for Security Studies, February 22, 2011.

International Crisis Group (ICG). *Lessons from Nigeria's 2011 Elections*, Africa Briefing 81. Abuja, Nigeria/Dakar, Senegal/Brussels, Belgium: ICG, September 15, 2011. Available from *www.crisisgroup.org/~/media/Files/africa/west-africa/nigeria/B81%20-%20Lessons%20from%20Nigeras%202011%20Elections.pdf*.

ICG. *Nigeria: Nigeria's Faltering Federal Experiment*, Africa Report 119. Abuja, Nigeria/Dakar, Senegal/Brussels, Belgium: ICG, October 25, 2006. Available from *www.crisisgroup.org/~/media/Files/africa/west-africa/nigeria/Nigerias%20Faltering%20Federal%20Experiment.pdf*.

ICG. *Nigeria: Seizing the Moment in the Niger Delta*, Africa Briefing 60. Abuja, Nigeria/Dakar, Senegal/Brussels, Belgium: ICG, April 30, 2009. Available from *www.crisisgroup.org/~/media/Files/africa/west-africa/nigeria/B060%20Nigeria%20Seizing%20the%20Moment%20in%20the%20Niger%20Delta.pdf*.

ICG. *Northern Nigeria: Background to Conflict*, Africa Report 168. Abuja Nigeria/Dakar, Senegal/Brussels, Belgium: ICG, December 20, 2010. Available from *www.crisisgroup.org/~/media/ Files/africa/west-africa/nigeria/168%20Northern%20Nigeria%20-%20 Background%20to%20Conflict.pdf.*

Jackson, Ashley. "Nigeria: A Security Overview." *The Round Table: Commonwealth Journal of International Affairs*, Vol. 96, No. 392, October 2007, pp. 587-603.

Jenne, Erin. "National Self-Determination A Deadly Mobilizing Device," in Hurst Hannum and Eileen F. Babbitt, eds., *Negotiating Self-Determination*, Boulder, CO: Lexington Book, 2006, pp. 7-36.

Katani, Parseleo. "Violence in Northern Nigeria Follows Goodluck Jonathan's Election Win." *Washington Post*, April 19, 2011. Available from *www.washingtonpost.com/world/violence-in-northern-nigeria-follows-goodluck-jonathans-election-win/2011/04/18/ AFQ4jx1D_story.html.*

Kenny, Joseph. "Facing Ethnicity and Religion: A Concern in Nigerian Education," in Ernest E. Uwaizie, Isaac O. Albert, and Godfrey N. Uzoigwe, eds., *Inter-Ethnic and Religious Conflict Resolution in Nigeria*, Lanham, MD: Lexington Books, 1999, pp. 49-56.

Kitson, A. E. *Southern Nigeria* map. London, UK: Royal Geographical Society, 1913.

Kreisher, Otto. "DOD Too Cautious: 'We Have to be Willing to Fail,' Says Flournoy." *AOL Defense.*, December 12, 2012. Available from *defense.aol.com/2012/12/12/dod-too-cautious-we-have -to-be-willing-to-fail-says-flournoy.*

Kwaja, Chris. "Nigeria's Pernicious Drivers of Ethno-Religious Conflict." *Africa Security Brief*, No. 14, July 2011. Available from *africacenter.org/wp-content/uploads/2011/06/AfricaBrief Final_14.pdf.*

Ladan, Muhammed Tawfiq. "The Role of Youth in Inter-Ethnic and Religious Conflicts: The Kaduna/Kano Case Study," in Ernest E. Uwaizie, Isaac O. Albert, and Godfrey N. Uzoigwe, eds.,

Inter-Ethnic and Religious Conflict Resolution in Nigeria. Lanham, MD: Lexington Books, 1999, pp. 98-111.

Lewis, Peter. "The Dysfunctional State of Nigeria," in Nancy Birdsall, Milan Vaishnav and Robert L. Ayres, eds., *Short of the Goal: U.S. Policy and Poorly Performing States,* Washington DC: Center for Global Development, 2006, pp. 83-116.

Lewis, Peter M. *Nigeria: Assessing Risks to Stability.* Washington DC: Center for Strategic and International Studies, June 2011. Available from *csis.org/files/publication/110623_Lewis_Nigeria_Web.pdf.*

Lloyd-Damnjanovic, Anastasya. "Governance, Security Among Areas of U.S.-Nigerian Cooperation." Washington DC: U.S. Department of State, June 7, 2012. Available from *www.africom.mil/getArticle.asp?art=7963.*

Lopez, C. Todd. "Dagger Brigade to 'Align' with AFRICOM." Army News Service, June 21, 2012. Available from *www.army.mil/article/82376/Dagger_Brigade_to__align__with_AFRICOM_in_2013/.*

McLoughlin, Gerald and Clarence Bouchat. *Nigerian Unity: In the Balance.* Carlisle, PA: Strategic Studies Institute, June 2013.

Morelli, Massimo and Dominic Rohner. "Natural Resource Distribution and Multiple Forms of Civil War." New York: Columbia University, August 9, 2010, pp. 1-30. Available from *humansecuritygateway.com/documents/NaturalResourceDistributionandMultipleFormsofCivilWar.pdf.*

Neary, Peter and Sweder Van Wijnbergen. *Natural Resources and the Macroeconomy. Cambridge.* Cambridge, MA: MIT Press, 1986.

Newsom, Chris. *Conflict in the Niger Delta: More than a Local Affair.* Washington DC: U.S. Institute of Peace, June 2011. Available from *www.usip.org/files/resources/Conflict_Niger_Delta.pdf.*

NgorNgor, Awunah Donald. "Effective Methods to Combat Transnational Organized Crime in Criminal Justice Processes: The Nigerian Perspective." 116th International Training Course Participants' Papers, Resource Material Series No. 58. Tokyo, Japan: The United Nations Asia and Far East Institute for the Prevention of Crime and the Treatment of Offenders (UNAFEI), December 2001. Available from *www.unafei.or.jp/english/pdf/PDF_rms/no58/58-13.pdf*.

"Niger Delta Call for 2011 Referendum: Secession, Stability, Socialism." *Niger Delta Now*, undated. Available from *nigerdeltanow.com/*.

"Nigeria Foreign Assistance." Washington DC: U.S. Department of State, 2012. Available from *foreignassistance.gov/OU.aspx?OUID=175&FY=2013&AgencyID=0&budTab=tab_Bud_Spent*.

Okonta, Ike. "Nigeria's Homegrown Terrorists." *Project Syndicate*, October 6, 2011. Available from *www.project-syndicate.org/commentary/okonta11/English?utm_medium=referral&utm_source=pulsenews*.

Olaniyi, Muideen *et al.* "Nigeria: Drums of Secession Sound From Niger Delta - Yakassai, Others Challenge Jonathan." *allAfrica*, August 12, 2012. Available from *allafrica.com/stories/201208120224.html*.

Odierno, Raymond T. *2012 Army Strategic Planning Guidance*. Washington DC: U.S. Department of the Army, April 19, 2012. Available from *usarmy.vo.llnwd.net/e2/c/downloads/243816.pdf*.

Osae-Brown, Anthony. "Mathematics of Winning the Presidential Polls." *Business Day*, April 14, 2011. Available from *www.businessdayonline.com/NG/index.php/news/111-politics/20483-mathematics-of-winning-the-presidential-polls*.

Ostebo, Terje. "Islamic Militancy in Africa." *Africa Security Brief*, No. 23, November 2012, pp. 1-8. Available from *africacenter.org/wp-content/uploads/2012/11/AfricaBriefFinal_23-2.pdf*.

Osumah, Oarhe and Augustine Ikelegbe. "The Peoples Democratic Party and Governance in Nigeria, 1999-2007." *Journal of*

Social Sciences, Vol. 19, No. 3, 2009, pp. 185-199. Available from *www.krepublishers.com/02-Journals/JSS/JSS-19-0-000-09-Web/JSS-19-3-000-09-Abst-PDF/JSS-19-3-185-2009-777-Osumah-O/JSS-19-3-185-2009-777-Osumah-O-Tt.pdf.*

Prendergast, Kenneth L. *Security Assistance in Nigeria: Shaping the International Environment to Meet U.S. National Security Objectives in the Global Era.* Carlisle, PA: U.S. Army War College, 2003.

Pryor Fredric L. *The Political Economy of Poverty, Equity, and Growth: Malawi and Madagasca*r. Oxford, UK: Oxford University Press, 1990.

Ratnikas, Algis. "Nigeria Timeline." *Timelines of History.* Available from *timelines.ws/countries/NIGERIA.HTML.*

Reno, William. "Shadow States and the Political Economy of Civil Wars," in Mats Berdal and David M. Malone, eds., *Greed and Grievance.* Boulder, CO: Lynne Rienner Publishers, 2000, pp. 44-66.

Reynolds, Jonathan T. "Nigeria and Shari'a: Religion and Politics in a West African Nation." *History Behind the Headlines*, Vol. 2, 2001, pp. 214-220.

Ringler, Kristine, Kathryn Coronges, and Chris Arney. "USMA's Minerva Research Initiative, Why Is Understanding Culture Important to the Military," *Phalanx*, September 2012. Available from *www.westpoint.edu/minerva/Shared_Minerva_Documents/September_2012-USMA_Minerva_MORS_Phalanx.pdf.*

Ross, Michael L. "The Political Economy of the Resource Curse." *World Politics*, Vol. 51, No. 2, January 1999, pp. 297-322.

Roulo, Claudette. "Dempsey: Forming Partnerships Vital for Future Force." American Forces Press Service, July 18, 2012. Available from *www.army.mil/article/83792/.*

Serafino, Nina M. "CRS Report for Congress Section 1206 of the National Defense Authorization Act for Fiscal Year 2006," *The DISAM Journal*, September 2008, pp. 19-25. Available from *www.disam.dsca.mil/pubs/Vol%2030_3/Serafino.pdf.*

Stewart, Scott. "Is Boko Haram More Dangerous than Ever?" *StratFor*, December 13, 2012. Available from *www.stratfor.com/weekly/boko-haram-more-dangerous-ever?utm_source=freelist-f&utm_medium=email&utm_campaign=20121213&utm_term=sweekly&utm_content=readmore&elq=fcb8c1a27ee34bf4851b3ec0f5b0bb22.*

Stewart, Scott. "The Rising Threat from Nigeria's Boko Haram Militant Group." *Stratfor*, November 10, 2011. Available from *www.stratfor.com/weekly/20111109-rising-threat-nigerias-boko-haram-militant-group?utm_source=freelist-f&utm_medium=email&utm_campaign=111110&utm_term=sweekly&utm_content=readmore&elq=a33db215cff347ffb5222bf4c45fb5d7.*

Topographic Section, General Staff. *Lagos and Southern Nigeria* map 2084. London, UK: War Office, General Staff, Topographical Section, 1905.

Transparency International (TI). "Corruption Perceptions Index 2011." Available from *cpi.transparency.org/cpi2011/results/.*

"U.S. Foreign Military Assistance, Program Descriptions." Washington, DC: Federation of American Scientists. Available from *www.fas.org/asmp/profiles/aid/aidindex.htm.*

Uwazie, Queen Florence. "The Emergence of Political Terrorism in Nigeria," in Ernest E. Uwaizie, Isaac O. Albert, and Godfrey N. Uzoigwe, eds., *Inter-Ethnic and Religious Conflict Resolution in Nigeria*. Lanham, MD: Lexington Books, 1999, pp. 113-119.

Uzoigwe, Godfrey N. "Assessing the History of Ethnic/Religious Relations," in Ernest E. Uwaizie, Isaac O. Albert, and Godfrey N. Uzoigwe, eds., *Inter-Ethnic and Religious Conflict Resolution in Nigeria*. Lanham, MD: Lexington Books, 1999, pp. 7-18.

Vandiver, John. "AFRICOM First to Test New Regional Brigade Concept." *Stars and Stripes*, May 17, 2012. Available from *www.stripes.com/news/africom-first-to-test-new-regional-brigade-concept-1.177476.*

Vergun, David. "Army Partnering for Peace, Security." U.S. Army New Service, October 25, 2012. Available from *www.army.mil/ article/90010/Army_partnering_for_peace__security/*.

Wadho, Waqar Ahmed. *Education, Rent-seeking and the Curse of Natural Resources.* MPRA Paper 37831. Munich: University Library of Munich, 2011. Available from *ideas.repec.org/p/pra/ mprapa/37831.html.*

Wuestner, Scott G. *Building Partner Capacity/Security Force Assistance: A New Structural Paradigm."* Carlisle, PA: Strategic Studies Institute, 2009. Available from *www.strategicstudiesinstitute.army.mil/pubs/display.cfm?pubID=880.*

Yakuba, J. Ademola. "Ethnicity and the Nigerian Constitutions," in Ernest E. Uwaizie, Isaac O. Albert, and Godfrey N. Uzoigwe, eds., *Inter-Ethnic and Religious Conflict Resolution in Nigeria.* Lanham, MD: Lexington Books, 1999, pp. 37-48.

"Yoruba Leaders Call for Regional Autonomy, Not Secession." *allAfrica,* September 4, 2012. Available from *allafrica.com/ stories/201209050274.html.*

ENDNOTES

1. Central Intelligence Agency (CIA), *The 2012 World Factbook*, 2012, Nigeria, available from *https://www.cia.gov/library/publications/the-world-factbook/geos/ni.html*.

2. Kenneth L. Prendergast, *Security Assistance in Nigeria: Shaping the International Environment to Meet U.S. National Security Objectives in the Global Era*, Carlisle, PA: U.S. Army War College, 2003, p. 14; Michael A. Blessing, *Nigeria's Center(s) of Gravity; A Complex and Violent Operational Environment*, Carlisle, PA: U.S. Army War College, 2008, p. 11, available from *www.dtic.mil/cgi-bin/GetTRDoc?AD=ADA478387&Location=U2&doc=GetTRDoc.pdf*; and Thomas Dempsey, "The Transformation of African Militaries," in Amy Krakowka and Laurel Hummel, eds., *Understanding Africa: A Geographic Approach*, West Point, NY: United States Military Academy, 2009, pp. 387-391, especially p. 390.

3. CIA, Nigeria.

4. International Crisis Group (ICG), *Nigeria: Nigeria's Faltering Federal Experiment*, Africa Report 119, Abuja, Nigeria/Dakar, Senegal/Brussels, Belgium: ICG, October 25, 2006, pp. 12-13, available from *www.crisisgroup.org/~/media/Files/africa/west-africa/nigeria/Nigerias%20Faltering%20Federal%20Experiment.pdf*.

5. CIA, Nigeria; Oarhe Osumah and Augustine Ikelegbe: "The Peoples Democratic Party and Governance in Nigeria, 1999-2007," *Journal of Social Sciences*, Vol. 19, No. 3, 2009, p. 196, available from *www.krepublishers.com/02-Journals/JSS/JSS-19-0-000-09-Web/JSS-19-3-000-09-Abst-PDF/JSS-19-3-185-2009-777-Osumah-O/JSS-19-3-185-2009-777-Osumah-O-Tt.pdf*; and Adekeye Adebajo, *The Curse of Berlin: Africa after the Cold War*, New York: Columbia University Press, 2010, p. 124.

6. Peter Lewis, "The Dysfunctional State of Nigeria," in Nancy Birdsall, Milan Vaishnav and Robert L. Ayres, eds., *Short of the Goal: U.S. Policy and Poorly Performing States*, Washington DC: Center for Global Development, 2006, pp. 83-116, especially pp. 103-104.

7. Adebajo, p. 124.

8. Department of Defense (DoD) and Department of State (DoS), *Foreign Military Training and DoD Engagement Activities of Interest, 2009-10,* Washington, DC: U.S. DoD and DoS, 2010, available from *www.state.gov/t/pm/rls/rpt/fmtrpt/.*

9. Simeon H. O. Alozieuwa, "Beyond the Ethno-Religious Theory of the Jos Conflict," *Africa Peace and Conflict Journal,* Vol. 3, No. 2, 2010, p. 23, available from *www.apcj.upeace.org/issues/APCJ_Dec2010_Vol3_Num2.pdf.*

10. Fredric L. Pryor, *The Political Economy of Poverty, Equity, and Growth: Malawi and Madagascar,* Oxford, UK: Oxford University Press, 1990, p. 12.

11. George Friedman, "Financial Markets, Politics, and the New Reality," *Stratfor,* August 7, 2012, available from *www.stratfor.com/weekly/financial-markets-politics-and-new-reality?utm_source=freelist-f&utm_medium=email&utm_campaign=20120807&utm_term=gweekly&utm_content=readmore&elq=190331b653e84cbb9fd56af99a9be15a.*

12. *Ibid.*

13. William Reno, "Shadow States and the Political Economy of Civil Wars," in Mats Berdal and David M. Malone, eds., *Greed and Grievance,* Boulder, CO: Lynne Rienner Publishers, 2000, pp. 44-66, especially p. 44.

14. Clarence Bouchat, "The North-South Divide within Mediterranean Countries," *Mediterranean Quarterly,* Vol. 5, No. 1, Fall 1994, pp. 128-132.

15. Waqar Ahmed Wadho, *Education, Rent-seeking and the Curse of Natural Resources,* MPRA Paper 37831, Munich, Germany: University Library of Munich, 2011, p. 2, available from *ideas.repec.org/p/pra/mprapa/37831.html.*

16. Note: The use of GDP purchasing power parity (PPP) is a relatively new method of measuring a country's economic production, rather than the previous method of calculating GDP based upon a set exchange rate. PPP measurements reduce the error that transitory U.S. dollar (the usual medium used to ensure like

comparisons) exchange rate spikes induce and accounts for the difficulty in obtaining common basic necessities for living. Using the GDP PPP usually increases the amount of economic production per person in lesser-developed countries, thereby reducing the perception of poverty suffered when compared to unadjusted figures. Since this comparison starts with figures computed with the official exchange rate at the time, a GDP per capita of $1,470 based on the 2010 official exchange rate is also used. The bottom line is that the average share of a Nigerian's slice of the country's economic pie has remained stagnant over 40 years, and dipped considerably in the interim, despite Nigeria's enormous natural resource wealth. The GDP PPP in Nigeria for 2010 is $2,500, ranking it 175th lowest in the world. CIA, Nigeria.

17. Toyin Falola, *The History of Nigeria*, Westport, CT: Greenwood Press, 1999, p. 16; and Juliet Elu: "Human Development in Sub-Sahara Africa: Analysis and Prospects for the Future," *Journal of Third World Studies*, Vol. 17, No. 2, Fall 2000, p. 53.

18. CIA, Nigeria.

19. James Butty, "Nigerian Professor Says Latest Jos Violence a Result of Many Factors," *VOANews.com*, January 18, 2010, available from *www.voanews.com/content/butty-nigeria-violence-analysis-20jan10-82131892/152914.html*.

20. David Bevan, Paul Collier, and Jan Willem Gunning, *The Political Economy of Poverty, Equity, and Growth: Nigeria and Indonesia*, Oxford, UK: Oxford University Press, 1999, p. 189; and Lewis, "The Dysfunctional State of Nigeria," p. 83.

21. Ashley Jackson, "Nigeria: A Security Overview," *The Round Table: Commonwealth Journal of International Affairs*, Vol. 96, No. 392, October 2007, pp. 588-589.

22. N. I. Ikpeze, C. C. Soludo, and N. N. Elekwa, "Nigeria: The Political Economy of the Policy Process, Policy Choice, and Implementation," in Charles Chukwuma Soludo, Michael Osita Ogbu, and Ha-Joon Chang, eds., *The Politics of Trade and Industrial Policy in Africa: Forced Consensus?* Trenton, NJ: Africa World Press, 2004, pp. 341-364, especially p. 349.

23. Erin Jenne, "National Self-Determination A Deadly Mobilizing Device," in Hurst Hannum and Eileen F. Babbitt, eds., *Negotiating Self-Determination*, Boulder, CO: Lexington Book, 2006, pp. 7-36, especially pp. 7-8.

24. Peter M. Lewis, *Nigeria: Assessing Risks to Stability*, Washington DC: Center for Strategic and International Studies, June 2011, p. 8, available from *csis.org/files/publication/110623_Lewis_Nigeria_Web.pdf*.

25. Lewis, "The Dysfunctional State of Nigeria," p. 85.

26. CIA, Nigeria.

27. *Ibid.*

28. Falola, *History of Nigeria*, p. 138; and CIA, Nigeria.

29. Falola, *History of Nigeria*, p. 112.

30. Ikpeze, Soludo, and Elekwa, p. 341; and Lewis, "The Dysfunctional State of Nigeria," p. 88.

31. CIA, Nigeria.

32. Lewis, *Nigeria: Assessing Risks to Stability*, p. 81; and "Dutch Disease" *Investopedia*, available from *www.investopedia.com/terms/d/dutchdisease.asp#ixzz253jLCVuk*.

33. Peter Neary and Sweder Van Wijnbergen, *Natural Resources and the Macroeconomy*, Cambridge, MA: MIT Press, 1986, pp. 10-11.

34. Lewis, *Nigeria: Assessing Risks to Stability*, p. 81; and Prendergast, p. 16.

35. Prendergast, p. 16; and CIA, Nigeria.

36. Bevan, Collier, and Gunning, p. 3.

37. Michael L. Ross: "The Political Economy of the Resource Curse," *World Politics*, Vol. 51, No. 2, January 1999, p. 310.

38. Charles H. Cutter, *Africa 2007*, Harpers Ferry, WV: Stryker-Post Publications, 2007, p. 91; Lewis, *Nigeria: Assessing Risks to Stability*, p. 81; Ross, p. 306; and Bevan, Collier, and Gunning, pp. 1-2.

39. Nahzeem Mimiko, "Between Yugoslavia and Czechoslovakia: The Abacha Coup, the National Conference, and Prospects for Peace and Democracy in Nigeria," *Social Justice,* Vol. 22, No. 3, Fall 1995, p. 129; and Lewis, "The Dysfunctional State of Nigeria," p. 98.

40. Bevan, Collier, and Gunning, p. 184; Falola, *History of Nigeria*, p. 132; Elu, p. 5.

41. Ikpeze, Soludo, and Elekwa, p. 341.

42. Falola, *History of Nigeria*, p. 132; Elu, p. 2; and *Comprehensive Report on U.S. Trade and Investment Policy Toward Sub-Saharan Africa and Implementation of the African Growth and Opportunity Act,* Office of the United States Trade Representative, Washington, DC: DoS, May 2007, p. 21.

43. Lewis, "The Dysfunctional State of Nigeria," p. 94.

44. Bevan, Collier, and Gunning, p. 4.

45. Lewis, *Nigeria: Assessing Risks to Stability*, p. 90; Elu, p. 54; and Bevan, Collier, and Gunning, p. 190.

46. Lewis, "The Dysfunctional State of Nigeria," p. 81; Lewis, *Nigeria: Assessing Risks to Stability*, p. 98.

47. Bevan, Collier, and Gunning, p. 185.

48. Adebajo, p. 124.

49. Ross, p. 310.

50. Elu, p. 54.

51. Thomas L. Friedman, *The World is Flat: A Brief History of the Twenty-first Century,* Basking Ridge, NJ: Farrar, Straus and Gi-

roux, 2005, pp. 460-461; and Bonnie Ayodele, "Silence on Climate Change and Natural Resources Conflict in Nigeria: The Niger Delta Region Experience," in Donald Anthony Mwiturubani and Jo-Ansie van Wyk, eds., *Climate Change and Natural Resources Conflicts in Africa*, Pretoria, South Africa: Institute for Security Studies, 2010, pp. 105-122, especially p. 111.

52. Wadho, p. 2.

53. Lewis, "The Dysfunctional State of Nigeria," p. 98.

54. Bevan, Collier, and Gunning, p. 4; and Toyin Falola, *Culture and Customs of Nigeria*, Westport, CT: Greenwood Press, 2001, pp. 103, 141.

55. Lewis, *Nigeria: Assessing Risks to Stability*, pp. 90, 97; and Falola, *Culture and Customs of Nigeria*, p. 208.

56. Transparency International, "Corruption Perceptions Index 2011," available from *cpi.transparency.org/cpi2011/results/*; Blessing, p. 17; and Falola, *Culture and Customs of Nigeria*, pp. 12-13.

57. Paul Collier and Anke Hoeffler, *The Political Economy of Secession*, Washington DC: World Bank Development Research Group, 2006, p. 5.

58. Lewis, "The Dysfunctional State of Nigeria," p. 97.

59. Ross, pp. 312, 317; Collier and Hoeffler, p. 5; and Ikpeze, Soludo, and Elekwa, p. 346.

60. Wadho, p. 3.

61. Ikpeze, Soludo, and Elekwa, p. 344.

62. Ayodele, p. 111.

63. Ikpeze, Soludo, and Elekwa, p. 344; and Bevan, Collier, and Gunning, p. 188.

64. Falola, *History of Nigeria*, p. 226; and ICG, *Nigeria: Nigeria's Faltering Federal Experiment*, p. 2.

65. Lewis, *Nigeria: Assessing Risks to Stability*, pp. 5-6; J. Ademola Yakuba, "Ethnicity and the Nigerian Constitutions," in Ernest E. Uwaizie, Isaac O. Albert, and Godfrey N. Uzoigwe, eds., *Inter-Ethnic and Religious Conflict Resolution in Nigeria*, Lanham, MD: Lexington Books, 1999, pp. 37-48, especially p. 39; Falola, *History of Nigeria*, pp. 92, 109.

66. Falola, *History of Nigeria*, pp. 133, 150; ICG, *Nigeria: Nigeria's Faltering Federal Experiment*, p. 5; Bevan, Collier, and Gunning, p. 189; and Lewis, *Nigeria: Assessing Risks to Stability*, p. 6.

67. Lewis, "The Dysfunctional State of Nigeria," p. 2.

68. ICG, *Nigeria: Nigeria's Faltering Federal Experiment*, pp. 5-6; and Lewis, *Nigeria: Assessing Risks to Stability*, pp. 10-12.

69. ICG, *Nigeria: Nigeria's Faltering Federal Experiment*, p. 9; and Ayodele, p. 111.

70. Falola, *History of Nigeria*, p. 226; and ICG, *Nigeria: Nigeria's Faltering Federal Experiment*, p. 2.

71. Ikpeze, Soludo, and Elekwa, pp. 341-343; Wadho, p. 2; and Ross, p. 298.

72. Lewis, *Nigeria: Assessing Risks to Stability*, p. 87; and Reno, p. 46.

73. Ross, p. 312; and Lewis, "The Dysfunctional State of Nigeria," p. 99.

74. Elu, p. 57.

75. Lewis, "The Dysfunctional State of Nigeria," p. 99.

76. Alozieuwa, p. 28; and Falola, *Culture and Customs of Nigeria*, p. 170.

77. Falola, *History of Nigeria,* p. 153; Falola, *Culture and Customs of Nigeria,* p. 13; and Salisu A. Abdullahi, "Ethnicity and Ethnic Relations in Nigeria: The Case of Religious Conflict in Kano," Judy Carter, George Irani and Vamik D. Volkan, eds., *Regional and Ethnic Conflicts: Perspectives from the Front Lines,* Upper Saddle River, NJ: Pearson Prentice Hall, 2009, pp. 292-299, especially p. 296.

78. Lewis, *Nigeria: Assessing Risks to Stability,* p. 9.

79. Alozieuwa, pp. 24, 27; and Abdullahi, p. 297.

80. Falola, *History of Nigeria,* p. 130; Falola, *Culture and Customs of Nigeria,* p. 21; Conerly Casey, "Mediated Hostility, Generation, and Victimhood in Northern Nigeria," Judy Carter, George Irani and Vamik D. Volkan, eds., *Regional and Ethnic Conflicts: Perspectives from the Front Lines,* Upper Saddle River, NJ: Pearson Prentice Hall, 2009, pp. 274-291, especially p. 276; and Wadho, p. 4.

81. Chris Newsom, *Conflict in the Niger Delta: More than a Local Affair,* Washington DC: U.S. Institute of Peace, June 2011, p. 9, available from *www.usip.org/files/resources/Conflict_Niger_Delta. pdf;* Falola, *Culture and Customs of Nigeria,* p. 164; and ICG, *Nigeria: Nigeria's Faltering Federal Experiment,* p. 9.

82. ICG, *Nigeria: Nigeria's Faltering Federal Experiment,* p. 9; Falola, *History of Nigeria,* p. 171; and Alozieuwa, p. 30.

83. Alozieuwa, p. 27; Falola, *History of Nigeria,* pp. 103, 170; and Chris Kwaja, "Nigeria's Pernicious Drivers of Ethno-Religious Conflict," *Africa Security Brief,* No. 14, July 2011, p. 1, available from *africacenter.org/wp-content/uploads/2011/06/AfricaBriefFinal_14.pdf.*

84. Lewis, "The Dysfunctional State of Nigeria," p. 99; Abdullahi, p. 298; Falola, *History of Nigeria,* p. 14; Ike Okonta, "Nigeria's Homegrown Terrorists," *Project Syndicate,* October 6, 2011, available from *www.project-syndicate.org/commentary/okonta11/ English?utm_medium=referral&utm_source=pulsenews;* and Ikpeze, Soludo, and Elekwa, p. 342.

85. Herman J. Cohen: "Africa: A Light at the End of the Tunnel?" *Air and Space Power Journal–Africa and Francophonie,* Vol. 1, No. 3, Fall 2010, pp. 11-12, available from *www.academyofdiplomacy.org/publications/article_archive/Africa%20by%20Cohen.pdf;* and Lewis, *Nigeria: Assessing Risks to Stability,* p. 96.

86. Ikpeze, Soludo, and Elekwa, pp. 341-342; and Lewis, *Nigeria: Assessing Risks to Stability,* pp. 89-90, 96.

87. Lewis, *Nigeria: Assessing Risks to Stability,* pp. 89-90.

88. Lewis, *Nigeria: Assessing Risks to Stability,* pp. 89-90; Ikpeze, Soludo, and Elekwa, p. 344; Falola, *Culture and Customs of Nigeria,* p. 227.

89. Blessing, p. 17.

90. Osumah and Ikelegbe, pp. 197-198.

91. April A. Gordon and Donald L. Gordon, "Trends and Prospects," Gordon and Gordon, eds., *Understanding Contemporary Africa,* Boulder, CO: Lynne Reinner Publishers, 2007, pp. 399-400.

92. Transparency International.

93. Falola, *History of Nigeria,* pp. 169-174; and Falola, *Culture and Customs of Nigeria,* pp. 22-24.

94. Stephen Ellis, "The Roots of African Corruption," *Current History,* Vol. 105, No. 691, May 2006, p. 204; and Ikpeze, Soludo, and Elekwa, p. 345.

95. Okonta.

96. Isaac O. Albert, "The Sociocultural Politics of Ethnic and Religious Conflicts," Ernest E. Uwaizie, Isaac O. Albert, and Godfrey N. Uzoigwe, eds., *Inter-Ethnic and Religious Conflict Resolution in Nigeria,* Lanham, MD: Lexington Books, 1999, pp. 70-87, especially pp. 70, 77; and Kwaja, p. 1.

97. Osumah and Ikelegbe, p. 189.

98. "Nigeria," Washington DC: U.S. Department of Energy, Energy Information Administration (EIA), August 2011, available from *www.eia.gov/countries/cab.cfm?fips=NI.*

99. Victor-Yves Ghebadi, "CSSM — A Chance for Peace in the Middle East," *International Defense Review*, February 1992, p. 118; LaVerle Berry, "The Society and Its Environment," in *Algeria, A Country Study*, Washington DC: Department of the Army, 1985, p. 105; and Lewis, *Nigeria: Assessing Risks to Stability*, pp. 9-10.

100. Ikpeze, Soludo, and Elekwa, p. 345; Lewis, *Nigeria: Assessing Risks to Stability*, p. 5; Albert, "The Sociocultural Politics of Ethnic and Religious Conflicts," p. 81; Falola, *History of Nigeria*, p. 91; Kwaja, pp. 2-4; and Alozieuwa, pp. 29-30.

101. ICG, *Nigeria: Nigeria's Faltering Federal Experiment*, pp. 12-13; and ICG, *Northern Nigeria: Background to Conflict*, Africa Report 168, Abuja, Nigeria/Dakar, Senegal/Brussels, Belgium: ICG, December 20, 2010, p. 20, available from *www.crisisgroup.org/~/media/ Files/africa/west-africa/nigeria/168%20Northern%20Nigeria%20-%20 Background%20to%20Conflict.pdf.*

102. Otive Igbuzor, "Nigeria's Experience in Managing the Challenges of Ethnic and Religious Diversity through Constitutional Provisions," Ethnic Nationalities Council, Burma, 2012, available from *www.encburma.net/index.php/feature/54-feature/166-nigerias-experience-in-managing-the-challenges-of-ethnic-a-religious-diversity-through-constitutional-provisions.html*; Adebajo, p. 134; and Lewis, *Nigeria: Assessing Risks to Stability*, p. 2.

103. ICG, *Northern Nigeria: Background to Conflict*, p. 21.

104. Terje Ostebo: "Islamic Militancy in Africa," *Africa Security Brief*, No. 23, November 2012, p. 2, available from *africacenter. org/wp-content/uploads/2012/11/AfricaBriefFinal_23-2.pdf*; and Falola, *Culture and Customs of Nigeria*, p. 44.

105. These nine states are joined by three more with partial implementation and include Bauchi, Borno, Gombe, Jigawa, Kaduna, Kano, Katsina, Kebbi, Niger, Sokoto, Yobe, and Zamfara. See ICG, *Northern Nigeria: Background to Conflict*, p. 1.

106. Falola, *History of Nigeria*, p. 32; ICG *Northern Nigeria: Background to Conflict*, p. 13; Falola, *Culture and Customs of Nigeria*, pp. 24-25; Kwaja, p. 5; and Muhammad Sani Umar, "Weak States and Democratization: Ethnic and Religious Conflicts in Nigeria," J. Craig Jenkins and Esther E. Gottlieb, eds., *Identity Conflicts: Can Violence by Regulated?* New Brunswick, NJ: Transaction Publishers, 2007, p. 268.

107. Jonathan T. Reynolds: "Nigeria and Shari'a: Religion and Politics in a West African Nation," *History Behind the Headlines*, Vol. 2, 2001, p. 215.

108. *Ibid.*, p. 217; and Falola, *History of Nigeria*, pp. 29-31.

109. ICG, *Nigeria: Nigeria's Faltering Federal Experiment*, p. i; and Reynolds, p. 217.

110. Falola, *Culture and Customs of Nigeria*, p. 40; ICG, *Nigeria: Nigeria's Faltering Federal Experiment*, pp. i, 6, 24; Abdullahi, p. 293; Lewis, *Nigeria: Assessing Risks to Stability*, p. 11; and Ostebo, p. 2.

111. ICG, *Northern Nigeria: Background to Conflict*, p. 20.

112. Scott Stewart, "Is Boko Haram More Dangerous than Ever?" *Stratfor*, December 13, 2012, available from *www.stratfor. com/weekly/boko-haram-more-dangerous-ever?utm_source=freelist-f&utm_medium=email&utm_campaign=20121213&utm_term=sweekly&utm_content=readmore&elq=fcb8c1a27ee34bf4851b3ec 0f5b0bb22.*

113. Ostebo, p. 2; and Scott Stewart, "The Rising Threat from Nigeria's Boko Haram Militant Group," *Stratfor*, November 10, 2011, available from *www.stratfor.com/weekly/20111109-rising-threat-nigerias-boko-haram-militant-group?utm_source=freelist-f&utm_medium=email&utm_campaign=111110&utm_term=sweekly&utm_content=readmore&elq=a33db215cff347ffb5222bf 4c45fb5d7.*

114. Stewart, "The Rising Threat from Nigeria's Boko Haram Militant Group"; and ICG, *Northern Nigeria: Background to Conflict*, pp. i, 20.

115. ICG, *Nigeria: Nigeria's Faltering Federal Experiment*, p. 13.

116. Alozieuwa, p. 25.

117. Falola, *Culture and Customs of Nigeria*, p. 40.

118. ICG, *Northern Nigeria: Background to Conflict*, pp. 13, 20.

119. ICG, *Northern Nigeria: Background to Conflict*, p. 21; Casey, p. 276.

120. Falola, *History of Nigeria*, p. 32; and ICG, *Northern Nigeria: Background to Conflict*, p. 22.

121. Abdullahi, p. 292; Falola, *Culture and Customs of Nigeria*, pp. 19, 28; and ICG, *Nigeria: Nigeria's Faltering Federal Experiment*, p. 3.

122. ICG, *Nigeria: Nigeria's Faltering Federal Experiment*, p. 3; ICG, *Northern Nigeria: Background to Conflict*, p. 5; and Alozieuwa, p. 22.

123. Falola, *Culture and Customs of Nigeria*, p. 36; Ostebo, p. 3; and Stewart, "Is Boko Haram More Dangerous than Ever?"

124. Ostebo, p. 3; Alozieuwa, p. 22.

125. Falola, *Culture and Customs of Nigeria*, p. 49; and Abdullahi, p. 296.

126. ICG, *Lessons from Nigeria's 2011 Elections*, Africa Briefing 81, Abuja, Nigeria/Dakar, Senegal/Brussels, Belgium: ICG, September 15, 2011, pp. 7-8, available from *www.crisisgroup.org/~/media/Files/africa/west-africa/nigeria/B81%20-%20Lessons%20from%20Nigeras%202011%20Elections.pdf*; Falola, *History of Nigeria*, p. 168; and Osumah and Ikelegbe, p. 189.

127. ICG, *Northern Nigeria: Background to Conflict*, p. ii; and Abdullahi, p. 296.

128. Alozieuwa, p. 20; Igbuzor; Falola, *Culture and Customs of Nigeria*, p. 49.

129. Lewis, "The Dysfunctional State of Nigeria," p. 97.

130. Falola, *Culture and Customs of Nigeria*, p. 91.

131. *Ibid.*, p. 168.

132. *Ibid.*, p. 43.

133. *Ibid.*, p. 124.

134. *Ibid.*, p. 187.

135. The usual ranges of 200 to 300 ethnic groups are given, based on definitions using language, customs, history, ancestry, foods, social organization, settlement patterns, and location among other characteristics. The website available from *www.onlinenigeria.com/tribes* lists 371 tribes by name and location.

136. Falola, *Culture and Customs of Nigeria*, pp. 4, 6; Alozieuwa, p. 26; ICG, *Northern Nigeria: Background to Conflict*, p. 2; and Abdullahi, p. 292.

137. Christopher Hewitt and Tom Cheetham, *Encyclopedia of Modern Separatist Movements*, Santa Barbara, CA: ABC-CLIO, 2000, p. 206; Falola, *Culture and Customs of Nigeria*, p. 5; and Blessing, p. 18.

138. Muhammed Tawfiq Ladan, "The Role of Youth in Inter-Ethnic and Religious Conflicts: The Kaduna/Kano Case Study," Ernest E. Uwaizie, Isaac O. Albert, and Godfrey N. Uzoigwe, eds., *Inter-Ethnic and Religious Conflict Resolution in Nigeria*, Lanham, MD: Lexington Books, 1999, pp. 98-111, especially p. 98.

139. Hewitt and Cheetham, p. 206; and Falola, *Culture and Customs of Nigeria*, p. 167.

140. Matthew Todd Bradley: "Inter-Ethnic Antagonism in Post-Colonial Nigeria: Ethnicity vs. Symbolic Nationalism," *Journal of Cultural Studies*, Vol. 7, No. 1, 2006, p. 71; Osumah and Ikelegbe, p. 189; and Falola, *Culture and Customs of Nigeria*, p. 91.

141. Osumah and Ikelegbe, p. 189; and ICG, *Nigeria: Nigeria's Faltering Federal Experiment,* p. 2.

142. Lewis, "The Dysfunctional State of Nigeria," p. 97.

143. Bradley, p. 71; Falola, *Culture and Customs of Nigeria,* pp. 99, 224; and Lewis, *Nigeria: Assessing Risks to Stability,* p. 7.

144. Falola, *Culture and Customs of Nigeria,* p. 104.

145. Collier and Hoeffler, p. 17.

146. Hewitt and Cheetham, p. 45; American School of International Service, "The Biafran War," Washington DC: American University School of International Service, November 1997, available from *www1.american.edu/ted/ice/biafra.htm*; and Reynolds, p. 215.

147. Adebola Ekanola, "National Integration and the Survival of Nigeria in the 21st Century," *The Journal of Social, Political, and Economic Studies,* Vol. 31, Fall 2006, p. 287; and Bradley, p. 71.

148. Sec. 202 of the constitution of the Second Republic, sec. 220 of the 1989 constitution, and sec. 221 of the constitution of the Fourth Republic. All three constitutions also ban the formation of any religion as a state religion in sec. 10, 11, and 10, respectively. Sec. 125-6, 130-2, and 131-4, respectively, govern the requirements for multiregional support for the election of the president as described in Igbuzor.

149. Anthony Osae-Brown, "Mathematics of Winning the Presidential Polls," *Business Day,* April 14, 2011, available from *www.businessdayonline.com/NG/index.php/news/111-politics/20483-mathematics-of-winning-the-presidential-polls*; Igbuzor; and Falola, *Culture and Customs of Nigeria,* p. 163.

150. Igbuzor; and Lewis, *Nigeria: Assessing Risks to Stability,* p. 8.

151. Umar, p. 265; Abdullahi, p. 295; and Kwaja, p. 2.

152. Osumah and Ikelegbe, p. 197.

153. Newsom, p. 5; Falola, *Culture and Customs of Nigeria*, p. 25; and ICG, *Nigeria: Nigeria's Faltering Federal Experiment*, pp. 8, 16.

154. Blessing, p. 18; ICG, *Nigeria: Nigeria's Faltering Federal Experiment*, pp. 5-6; and Lewis, *Nigeria: Assessing Risks to Stability*, pp. 10-12.

155. Akpomuvie Orhioghene Benedict, "Breaking Barriers to Transformation of the Niger Delta Region of Nigeria: A Human Development Paradigm," *Journal of Sustainable Development*, Vol. 4, No. 3, June 2011, p. 211; ICG, *Nigeria: Nigeria's Faltering Federal Experiment*, pp. 5-6; Lewis, *Nigeria: Assessing Risks to Stability*, pp. 10-12; and Collier and Hoeffler, p. 18.

156. Stewart, "The Rising Threat from Nigeria's Boko Haram Militant Group."

157. Casey, p. 285; Queen Florence Uwazie, "The Emergence of Political Terrorism in Nigeria," Ernest E. Uwaizie, Isaac O. Albert, and Godfrey N. Uzoigwe, eds., *Inter-Ethnic and Religious Conflict Resolution in Nigeria*, Lanham, MD: Lexington Books, 1999, pp. 113-119, especially pp. 116-117; Igbuzor; and Reno, p. 51.

158. Abdullahi, p. 295.

159. Algis Ratnikas, "Nigeria Timeline," *Timelines of History*, available from *timelines.ws/countries/NIGERIA.HTML*.

160. Stewart, "Is Boko Haram More Dangerous than Ever?"

161. Kwaja, p. 2.

162. *Ibid.*, p. 2; and ICG, *Nigeria: Nigeria's Faltering Federal Experiment*, p. 12.

163. ICG, *Nigeria: Nigeria's Faltering Federal Experiment*, pp. 3-4, 12.

164. Alozieuwa, pp. 29-30.

165. Kwaja, p. 3.

166. *Ibid.*, p. 2.

167. Alozieuwa, pp. 29-30; Kwaja, p. 3; and ICG, *Nigeria: Nigeria's Faltering Federal Experiment*, p. 13.

168. Alozieuwa, p. 25.

169. ICG, *Nigeria: Nigeria's Faltering Federal Experiment*, p. 13.

170. *Ibid.*, p. 4.

171. *Ibid.*, p. 13.

172. Kwaja, pp. 3-4; and ICG, *Nigeria: Nigeria's Faltering Federal Experiment*, p. 13.

173. Kwaja, p. 3.

174. Igbuzor; and Reynolds, p. 217.

175. Osae-Brown.

176. Albert, "The Sociocultural Politics of Ethnic and Religious Conflicts," p. 70.

177. ICG, *Nigeria: Nigeria's Faltering Federal Experiment*, p. 11.

178. ICG, *Northern Nigeria: Background to Conflict*, p. 1.

179. The geopolitical zones are northeast, northwest, north-central, southeast, southwest, and south-south (or the Niger Delta area) for the positions of president, vice president, prime minister, deputy prime minister, senate president, and house speaker. This system was nearly made part of the constitution in the 1990s under General Abacha (Abdullahi, p. 292; Falola, *Culture and Customs of Nigeria*, pp. 200-202). The dominant ruling People's Democratic Party reconstituted the system within its ranks, but that now seems discarded, too (ICG, *Lessons from Nigeria's 2011 Elections*, p. 8).

180. Lewis, *Nigeria: Assessing Risks to Stability*, p. 9; Yakuba, p. 40; Parseleo Katani: "Violence in Northern Nigeria Follows Goodluck Jonathan's Election Win," *Washington Post*, April 19, 2011, available from *www.washingtonpost.com/world/violence-in-northern-nigeria-follows-goodluck-jonathans-election-win/2011/04/18/AFQ4jx1D_story.html*; and ICG, *Lessons from Nigeria's 2011 Elections*, p. 8.

181. Department of State, "Nigeria," *Background Notes*, Washington DC: DoS, Bureau of African Affairs, April 2012, available from *www.state.gov/r/pa/ei/bgn/2836.htm*; and Katani.

182. ICG, *Nigeria: Nigeria's Faltering Federal Experiment*, p. 5; and Alozieuwa, p. 23.

183. Ikpeze, Soludo, and Elekwa, p. 343.

184. Alozieuwa, p. 24.

185. Ikpeze, Soludo, and Elekwa, p. 345.

186. Elizabeth Crighton and Martha Abele MacIver, "The Evolution of Protracted Ethnic Conflict," *Comparative Politics*, Vol. 23, January 1991, p. 128.

187. Falola, *Culture and Customs of Nigeria*, pp. 5, 217, 227.

188. Bevan, Collier, and Gunning, p. 2.

189. Abdullahi, p. 295.

190. Bevan, Collier, and Gunning, pp. 5, 187.

191. Concerned African Scholars Organization, "U.S. Military Involvement in Nigeria," African Security Research Project, September 2009, available from *concernedafricascholars.org/african-security-research-project/?p=83*.

192. Falola, *History of Nigeria*, pp. 122, 129; Lewis, *Nigeria: Assessing Risks to Stability*, pp. 5-6; and Yakuba, p. 39.

193. Falola, *Culture and Customs of Nigeria*, p. 5.

194. Lewis, *Nigeria: Assessing Risks to Stability*, p. 1.

195. Yakuba, p. 39; and Falola, *History of Nigeria*, pp. 92, 109, 122.

196. ICG, *Nigeria: Nigeria's Faltering Federal Experiment*, p. 71; Godfrey N. Uzoigwe, "Assessing the History of Ethnic/Religious Relations," Ernest E. Uwaizie, Isaac O. Albert, and Godfrey N. Uzoigwe, eds., *Inter-Ethnic and Religious Conflict Resolution in Nigeria*, Lanham, MD: Lexington Books, 1999, pp. 7-18, especially p. 16; and Falola, *History of Nigeria*, p. 11.

197. Falola, *History of Nigeria*, p. 129.

198. *Ibid.*, p. 109; and Bevan, Collier, and Gunning, p. 188.

199. Bevan, Collier, and Gunning, p. 188.

200. Falola, *Culture and Customs of Nigeria*, p. 155; and ICG, *Nigeria: Nigeria's Faltering Federal Experiment*, p. 2.

201. Lewis, *Nigeria: Assessing Risks to Stability*, p. 88.

202. Collier and Hoeffler, p. 18.

203. *Ibid.*, pp. 3-5, 8.

204. Reynolds, p. 215; Muideen Olaniyi *et al.*, "Nigeria: Drums of Secession Sound From Niger Delta - Yakassai, Others Challenge Jonathan," *allAfrica*, August 12, 2012, available from *allafrica.com/stories/201208120224.html*; "Niger Delta Call for 2011 Referendum: Secession, Stability, Socialism," *Niger Delta Now*, undated, available from *nigerdeltanow.com/*; and ICG, *Nigeria: Nigeria's Faltering Federal Experiment*, p. 16.

205. Falola, *Culture and Customs of Nigeria*, pp. 217, 227; "Yoruba Leaders Call for Regional Autonomy, Not Secession," *allAfrica*, September 4, 2012, available from *allafrica.com/stories/201209050274.html*; and Massimo Morelli and Dominic Rohner, "Natural Resource Distribution and Multiple Forms of Civil War," New York: Columbia University, August 9, 2010, pp.

16-18, available from *econ.columbia.edu/files/econ/natural_resource_distribution__multiple_forms_of_civil_war.pdf.*

206. "Niger Delta Call for 2011 Referendum: Secession, Stability, Socialism."

207. ICG, *Nigeria: Nigeria's Faltering Federal Experiment*, p. 1.

208. Collier and Hoeffler, p. 18.

209. Benedict, p. 211; and Casey, p. 276.

210. Collier and Hoeffler, pp. 9, 14.

211. *Ibid.*, p. 18.

212. Jenne, p. 7; and Paul Collier and Nicholas Sambanis, "Understanding Civil War: A New Agenda," *Journal of Conflict Resolution*, Vol. 46, No. 1, February 2002, pp. 3–12.

213. Adebajo, p. 328.

214. Institute for Security Studies Seminar Report, *South Sudan's Referendum – Geopolitical and Geostrategic Implications*, New Muckleneuk, South Africa: Institute for Security Studies, February 22, 2011, pp. 2-3.

215. Maurice Iroulor Imoh, *The Development of an Atlas of the Nigerian Political Evolution*, Masters Degree Thesis, Columbus, OH: The Ohio State University, 1977, pp. 49-50; Ben Cahoon, "World Statesman – Nigeria," 2000, available from *www.world-statesmen.org/Nigeria.htm#Northern-Nigeria;* and Falola, *Culture and Customs of Nigeria*, p. 17.

216. Imoh, 49-50.

217. Cahoon; and Imoh, pp. 53-58.

218. Imoh, pp. 49-50; and Falola, *Culture and Customs of Nigeria*, p. 72.

219. Cahoon; and Imoh, pp. 53-58.

220. Falola, *Culture and Customs of Nigeria,* pp. 17, 68; and Imoh, pp. 49-60.

221. Topographic Section, General Staff, *Lagos and Southern Nigeria* map 2084, London, UK: War Office, General Staff, Topographical Section, 1905; Samuel Aryeetey Atoh, "Africa South of the Sahara," Douglas S. Johnson, Viola Haarmann, Merrill L. Johnson, and David L. Clawson, eds., *World Regional Geography,* Upper Saddle Brook, NJ: Pearson Prentice Hall, 2010, pp. 400-465, especially p. 438; Imoh, pp. 53-54; and A. E. Kitson, *Southern Nigeria* map, London, UK: Royal Geographical Society, 1913.

222. Imoh, pp. 53-58, 78-80, 88.

223. *Ibid,* p. 82; and Falola, *Culture and Customs of Nigeria,* p. 69.

224. Abdullahi, p. 295; and Toyin Falola and Matthew M. Heaton, "The Works of A. E. Afigbo on Nigeria: An Historigraphical Essay," *History in Africa,* Vol. 33, 2006, p. 159, available from *muse.jhu.edu/journals/hia/summary/v033/33.1falola.html.*

225. Imoh, pp. 47-53; Uzoigwe, p. 8; and ICG, *Northern Nigeria: Background to Conflict,* p. 20.

226. Benedict, p. 211.

227. Lewis, *Nigeria: Assessing Risks to Stability,* p. 3.

228. *Field Manual (FM) 5-0, The Operations Process,* Washington DC: U.S. Department of the Army, March 2010, p. 3-5.

229. Lewis, *Nigeria: Assessing Risks to Stability,* p. 85.

230. FM 5-0, pp. 3-5 to 3-6.

231. Lewis, "The Dysfunctional State of Nigeria," pp. 108-109.

232. Collier and Hoeffler.

233. Anastasya Lloyd-Damnjanovic, "Governance, Security Among Areas of U.S.-Nigerian Cooperation," Washing-

ton DC: DoS, June 7, 2012, available from *www.africom.mil/getArticle.asp?art=7963*; and Lewis, "The Dysfunctional State of Nigeria," p. 109.

234. Lewis, "The Dysfunctional State of Nigeria," pp. 106, 109.

235. Casey, p. 276.

236. Newsom, p. 3.

237. Fiscal Year 2013 Budget Estimates, Washington DC: Defense Security Cooperation Agency (DSCA), February 2012, p. 480, available from *comptroller.defense.gov/defbudget/fy2013/budget_justification/pdfs/01_Operation_and_Maintenance/O_M_VOL_1_PARTS/O_M_VOL_1_BASE_PARTS/DSCA_OP-5.pdf*.

238. Lewis, "The Dysfunctional State of Nigeria," pp. 106, 109.

239. Falola, *Culture and Customs of Nigeria*, p. 161.

240. Lewis, "The Dysfunctional State of Nigeria," p. 85.

241. Ostebo, p. 4.

242. Scott G. Wuestner, *Building Partner Capacity/Security Force assistance: A New Structural Paradigm,* Carlisle, PA: Strategic Studies Institute, 2009, p. 13, available from *www.strategicstudies institute.army.mil/pubs/display.cfm?pubID=880*.

243. Lewis, "The Dysfunctional State of Nigeria," p. 113.

244. Concerned African Scholars Organization.

245. Kristine Ringler, Kathryn Coronges, and Chris Arney, "USMA's Minerva Research Initiative, Why Is Understanding Culture Important to the Military," *Phalanx*, September 2012, p. 1, available from *www.westpoint.edu/minerva/Shared_Minerva_Documents/September_2012-USMA_Minerva_MORS_Phalanx.pdf*.

246. Lewis, "The Dysfunctional State of Nigeria," pp. 85-86.

247. Albert, "The Sociocultural Politics of Ethnic and Religious Conflicts," p. 73; and Abdullahi, p. 297.

248. Lewis, "The Dysfunctional State of Nigeria," p. 95.

249. Alozieuwa, p. 26; Falola, *Culture and Customs of Nigeria*, p. 107; and Falola and Heaton, p. 171.

250. Okonta; and Uzoigwe, p. 16.

251. Lewis, *Nigeria: Assessing Risks to Stability*, p. 17.

252. ICG, *Lessons from Nigeria's 2011 Elections 2011*, p. 20.

253. Kwaja, p. 7.

254. ICG, *Northern Nigeria: Background to Conflict*, p. 24.

255. Casey, p. 287.

256. Falola, *History of Nigeria*, p. 12.

257. Falola and Heaton, p. 172.

258. Falola, *Culture and Customs of Nigeria*, p. 27; Imoh, p. 47; and Falola and Heaton, pp. 157, 170-171.

259. Uzoigwe, p. 7.

260. Joseph Kenny,"Facing Ethnicity and Religion: A Concern in Nigerian Education," Ernest E. Uwaizie, Isaac O. Albert, and Godfrey N. Uzoigwe, eds., *Inter-Ethnic and Religious Conflict Resolution in Nigeria*, Lanham, MD: Lexington Books, 1999, pp. 49-56, especially p. 50.

261. Falola, *Culture and Customs of Nigeria*, p. 24.

262. Abdullahi, p. 292.

263. Imoh, p. 80.

264. This is more commonly known as "indirect rule." Lugard would formally record his ideas on Native Authority in his handbook, *The Dual Mandate in British Tropical Africa* (New York: League of Nations, 1922), while serving as British representative to the League of Nations' Permanent Mandates Commission.

265. Falola, *History of Nigeria*, p. 70.

266. Imoh, p. 88; and Falola and Heaton, p. 157.

267. Imoh, pp. 88, 92.

268. Adebajo,p. xiii.

269. *Ibid.*, p. 2.

270. Bevan, Collier, and Gunning, p. 189; and Albert, "The Sociocultural Politics of Ethnic and Religious Conflicts," p. 70.

271. Falola and Heaton, pp. 157, 162-164.

272. ICG, *Nigeria: Nigeria's Faltering Federal Experiment*, pp. 2-4.

273. Africa Center for Strategic Studies (ACSS), *2012 Workshop on Security Sector Reform/Transformation in West Africa*, Washington DC: ACSS, October 19, 2012, p. 17.

274. *Ibid.*, pp. 7-9.

275. Albert, "The Sociocultural Politics of Ethnic and Religious Conflicts," p. 70; Abdullahi, p. 298.

276. Lewis, "The Dysfunctional State of Nigeria," 2006, p. 107; and "Nigeria Foreign Assistance," Washington DC: DoS, 2012, available from *foreignassistance.gov/OU.aspx?OUID=175&FY=201 3&AgencyID=0&budTab=tab_Bud_Spent*.

277. ACSS, p. 4.

278. "Nigeria Foreign Assistance."

279. Lewis, "The Dysfunctional State of Nigeria," p. 110.

280. *Ibid.*

281. *U.S.-Nigeria Binational Commission Niger Delta and Security Cooperation Working Group Meeting on September 13-14,* Washington DC: U.S. Department of State, Office of the Spokesman, September 2010, available from *www.state.gov/r/pa/prs/ps/2010/09/147023. htm*; and U.S. Department of State, *U.S.-Nigeria Binational Commission Meets Regularly,* Washington DC: U.S. Department of State, Office of the Spokesman, November 2012, *www.state.gov/p/af/ci/ ni/139598.htm.*

282. Lloyd-Damnjanovic.

283. Gerald McLoughlin and Clarence Bouchat, *Nigerian Unity: In the Balance,* Carlisle, PA: Strategic Studies Institute, June 2013, p. 61; and Newsom, p. 2.

284. Concerned African Scholars Organization; and John Amoda, "Nigeria-U.S. Bi-National Commission and Nigeria Security Interest," *allAfrica,* October 15, 2012, available from *allafrica. com/stories/201210160458.html.*

285. *Field Manual (FM) 3-07.1, Security Force Assistance,* Washington DC: U.S. Department of the Army, May 2009, p. v, available from *usacac.army.mil/cac2/Repository/FM3071.pdf.*

286. The DoS use of the term "Stability Operations" as a subsector in this report includes peacekeeping, peace support, and humanitarian operations; coalition building; and security sector reform through training and operational support to military, police, and maritime forces. "Nigerian Foreign Assistance."

287. "Nigerian Foreign Assistance."

288. DoD and DoS, *Foreign Military Training and DOD Engagement Activities of Interest, 2009-10,* Vol. I, Sec III-I, p. 44.

289. Dempsey, pp. 387-391; *Ibid.*

290. DoD and DoS, *Foreign Military Training and DOD Engagement Activities of Interest, 2011-12,* Washington DC: DoD and DoS, 2012, Vol. I Sec IV-1, p. 52, available from *www.state.gov/t/pm/rls/rpt/fmtrpt/*.

291. *Ibid.,* Vol. I Sec III-I, p. 12.

292. *Nigeria: Seizing the Moment in the Niger Delta,* Africa Briefing No. 60, Abuja, Nigeria/Dakar, Senegal/Brussels, Belgium: ICG, April 30, 2009, p. 1, available from *www.crisisgroup.org/~/media/Files/africa/west-africa/nigeria/B060%20Nigeria%20Seizing%20 the%20Moment%20in%20the%20Niger%20Delta.pdf;* and Blessing, pp. 20-21.

293. "Nigeria Foreign Assistance."

294. *Ibid.*

295. Wuestner, pp. 29-30.

296. Blessing, pp. 20-21; and McLoughlin and Bouchat.

297. "U.S. Foreign Military Assistance, Program Descriptions," Washington, DC: Federation of American Scientists, available from *www.fas.org/asmp/profiles/aid/aidindex.htm*.

298. Uwazie, pp. 116-117.

299. Ostebo, p. 4; and Okonta.

300. "Nigerian Foreign Assistance."

301. Concerned African Scholars Organization; DoD and DoS, *Foreign Military Training and DOD Engagement Activities of Interest, 2011-12,* p. Vol. I Sec III-I, pp. 11-12; and Nina M. Serafino, "CRS Report for Congress Section 1206 of the National Defense Authorization Act for Fiscal Year 2006," *The DISAM Journal,* September 2008, p. 19, available from *www.disam.dsca.mil/pubs/Vol%2030_3/Serafino.pdf.*

302. DoD and DoS, *Foreign Military Training and DOD Engagement Activities of Interest, 2009-10,* Vol. I Sec III-I, p. 44; and Serafino, p. 19.

303. DoD and DoS, *Foreign Military Training and DOD Engagement Activities of Interest, 2011-12*, Vol. I Sec III-I, p. 12.

304. Ostebo, p. 1.

305. Awunah Donald NgorNgor, "Effective Methods to Combat Transnational Organized Crime in Criminal Justice Processes: The Nigerian Perspective," 116th International Training Course Participants' Papers, Resource Material Series No. 58, Tokyo, Japan: The United Nations Asia and Far East Institute for the Prevention of Crime and the Treatment of Offenders (UNAFEI), December 2001, pp. 173-176, available from *www.unafei.or.jp/english/pdf/PDF_rms/no58/58-13.pdf*.

306. *Ibid.*, p. 174.

307. "Nigeria Foreign Assistance."

308. Concerned African Scholars Organization; and NgorNgor, p. 181.

309. *The Management of Security Assistance*, Wright Patterson AFB, OH: Defense Institute of Security Assistance Management (DISAM), 2007, pp. 1-6, available from *www.disam.dsca.mil/documents/greenbook/v31/01_Chapter.pdf*.

310. DoD and DoS, *Foreign Military Training and DOD Engagement Activities of Interest, 2011-1*, Vol. I Sec III-I, p. 12.

311. ICG, *Nigeria: Seizing the Moment in the Niger Delta*, p. 5; Scott Baldauf, "Next Pirate Hot Spot: The Gulf of Guinea," *The Christian Science Monitor*, February 28, 2012, available from *www.csmonitor.com/World/Africa/2012/0228/Next-pirate-hot-spot-the-Gulf-of-Guinea*; and Concerned African Scholars Organization.

312. Baldauf.

313. Indeed, the U.S. Army has already jump-started the process of gaining regional expertise in a variety of other ways. Training and Doctrine Command (TRADOC) has formed the TRADOC Cultural Center (TCC), expanded operations at the

Defense Language Institute Foreign Language Center (DLIFLC), and developed the University of Foreign Military and Cultural Studies (UFMCS) (Wuestner, pp. 12-13). In September 2012, the Army also reopened the Military Accessions Vital to the National Interest (MAVINI) fast track to citizenship program meant to recruit native speakers in 47 languages, nine of which are spoken in Sub-Saharan Africa (including French, Portuguese, and Arabic), and three primarily in Nigeria (Hausa, Igbo, and Yoruba). Proper recruitment, management, and retention of so many selected skills will be a challenge to the Institutional Army, as it may already realize through managing its Special Forces Soldiers, and will require a sustained investment in money and resources (Griffin). Department of the Army, "MAVINI Information Sheet," Washington DC: U.S. Department of the Army, Office of the Assistant Secretary Manpower and Reserve Affairs, undated, available from *www.goarmy.com/content/dam/goarmy/downloaded_assets/mavni/mavni-language.pdf*; Steve Griffin, "Regionally-Aligned Brigades: There's More to This Plan Than Meets the Eye," *Small Wars Journal*, September 19, 2012, available from *smallwarsjournal.com/jrnl/art/regionally-aligned-brigades-theres-more-to-this-plan-than-meets-the-eye*; David Vergun, "Army Partnering for Peace, Security," U.S. Army News Service, October 25, 2012, available *www.army.mil/article/90010/Army_partnering_for_peace__security/*; and Dan Cox, "An Enhanced Plan for Regionally Aligning Brigades Using Human Terrain Systems," *Small Wars Journal*, June 14, 2012, available from *smallwarsjournal.com/jrnl/art/an-enhanced-plan-for-regionally-aligning-brigades-using-human-terrain-systems*.

314. John Vandiver, "AFRICOM First to Test New Regional Brigade Concept," Stars and Stripes, May 17, 2012, available from *www.stripes.com/news/africom-first-to-test-new-regional-brigade-concept-1177476*; and Vergun.

315. Wuestner, p. 17; and Griffin.

316. Otto Kreisher, "DOD Too Cautious: 'We Have to be Willing to Fail,' Says Flournoy," *AOL Defense.Com*, December 12, 2012, available from *defense.aol.com/2012/12/12/dod-too-cautious-we-have-to-be-willing-to-fail-says-flournoy*.

317. *Foreign Military Training and DOD Engagement Activities of Interest, 2009-10*, Vol. I Sec III-I, p. 44.

318. Raymond T. Odierno, *2012 Army Strategic Planning Guidance,* Washington DC: U.S. Department of the Army, April 19, 2012, p. 6, available from *usarmy.vo.llnwd.net/e2/c/downloads/243816.pdf.*

319. Wuestner, pp. 19-20.

320. Wuestner, p. 25; Vandiver; and Dave Dilegge, "USMC Forms MCTAG," *Small Wars Journal,* November 19, 2007, available from *smallwarsjournal.com/blog/usmc-forms-mctag.*

321. Claudette Roulo, "Dempsey: Forming Partnerships Vital for Future Force," American Forces Press Service, July 18, 2012, available from *www.army.mil/article/83792/.*

322. Vergun; C. Todd Lopez, "Dagger Brigade to 'align' with AFRICOM in 2013," Army News Service, June 21, 2012, available from *www.army.mil/article/82376/Dagger_Brigade_to_align_with_AFRICOM_in_2013/;* and Vandiver.

323. Wuestner, p. 30; and Vergun.

324. Griffin; and Cox.

325. Griffin.

326. *Ibid.;* and Wuestner, pp. 14-16, 36-37.

327. Griffin.

328. Lewis, "The Dysfunctional State of Nigeria," p. 112.

329. *Foreign Military Training and DOD Engagement Activities of Interest, 2011-12,* Vol. I Sec III-I, p. 12.

330. Lloyd-Damnjanovic.

331. ICG, *Northern Nigeria: Background to Conflict,* p. 24.

332. Lewis, "The Dysfunctional State of Nigeria," p. 100; and Judith Burdin Asuni, *Special Report: Blood Oil in the Niger Delta,* Washington DC: United States Institute of Peace, August 2009, p. 6.

333. *Foreign Military Training and DOD Engagement Activities of Interest, 2009-10*, Vol. I, Sect III-1, p. 44.

334. Wuestner, pp. 26-27, 37.

335. Amoda.

336. ACSS.

337. Concerned African Scholars Organization.

www.ingramcontent.com/pod-product-compliance
Lightning Source LLC
Chambersburg PA
CBHW070157290526
45789CB00002B/807